MY SEEDIE LIFE

Sowing Seeds of
Commitment and Cooperation

Ron Amarel

My Seedie Life
Sowing Seeds of Commitment and Cooperation

© 2022, Ron Amarel.

Print ISBN: 978-1-09837-4-723
eBook ISBN: 978-1-09837-4-730

CONTENTS

DEDICATION

I will always be thankful to my wife and family, and to the vegetable seed industry that provided the opportunities for me to work with great people and create long-lasting friendships.

I greatly appreciate the opportunities and people in my life. There were many that coached, supported, and provided me guidance along the way.

They are important to me and I would like to list them all. But too many to list, and they know who they are. I stay in touch with many today and their continued interaction is cherished.

God is mentioned in this book as a principal being of faith. My God may or not be your God which is respected and represents the individual faith, freedom and understanding we have for one another. Some of the topics may be mentioned twice or seem out of sequence but this is my life and I must say, it was not in perfect order.

"Though I do not believe that a plant will spring up where no seed has been, I have great faith in a seed. Convince me that you have a seed there, and I am prepared to expect wonders."

— Henry David Thoreau

INTRODUCTION

Most people spend a lifetime trying to figure out their purpose on Earth. For me, I found out early on. I was unquestionably put on this Earth to take care of the five ladies in my life; my wife, Lynette, and our four daughters, Rebecca, Terra, Carrie, and Ashlie. They always were and always will be the fuel that drives me to succeed, the inspiration that sparks my creativity, and the reason I constantly stretch for my fullest potential. I want to enable and provide for my family the very best that I can.

More than anything materialistic, I want to instill in my daughters (and now my grandchildren) the value of hard work, honesty, ingenuity, integrity and fairness. I want to live by example, just as I was shown at a young age by my own parents.

God provided me with the means to live this life. It's up to me to make it work. "Earning your keep" is what I like to call it, but whatever term you use, it's clear to me that life is what you make of it, and whenever you help someone, you're elevating everyone else in the process. It's a philosophy, provided to my family, that I take to work with me as well. I strive to earn respect and give people my very best in return for their support.

My ancestry has its roots firmly planted in the Azores, where commitment to family and community is valued. My own journey began in California, took me up to the Pacific Northwest, into Asia, through Africa, across Europe and over to South America. After living in many locations, we now call Middleton, Idaho our home.

Although I've had various titles, roles and responsibilities throughout my professional career, I'll always be a "seedsman" at heart. Seeds can provide the world with possibilities and seeds have provided a world of possibilities to me and my family. I always told my daughters as they were growing up to eat their vegetables as this was our lives. Vegetable seed, I would tell them, pay for the food on our table and your clothes – "Respect the power of a seed".

Whether I assessed them by cracking them between my teeth when I was young, or studied them under a microscope as I do now, it's still the seeds themselves that intrigue me—how to improve their strength, their yield, and their potential.

Whether it's the potential of a seed, or the potential of an idea. I'm always interested in enhancing their performance, looking toward the future to create a better way. Sure, we have to pay attention and learn from our history, but I can honestly say that I know more about tomorrow than I can tell you about yesterday.

I'm thankful to each and every "enabler"; those who have helped me to strive to do better. Perhaps, the best way I can honor them is to become an "enabler" myself.

I was taught and learned a lot of life and management lessons along the way. One of the most important and often, the most difficult, is when to decide for the silent many and not the vocal few. I cannot say I did this correct one hundred percent of the time, but I did my best to listen, study, and then, decide using the tools I learned through experience and training.

SOIL

"Soil is an almost magical substance, a living system
that transforms the materials it encounters."

— George Monbiot

"Essentially, all life depends upon the soil."

— Charles E. Kellogg

The Azores

I consider the Azores as my "soil." I am Portuguese with my ancestors' roots on both sides firmly planted in the Azores Islands; Pico on my mother's side and Sao Jorge on my father's side. My ancestors immigrated to California in the late 1920's and settled in Sacramento in the northern part of the state where both of my parents were born and raised.

My dad was fluent in Portuguese, but he raised us to speak English. He did not want us to have the difficulties he had when first joining school, not being fluent in English. Oh, I learned a couple words in Portuguese, but certainly nothing of the sort to carry on any kind of conversation, meaningful or otherwise. Even though my dad understood Portuguese well, he chose to speak English. It made for some amusing conversations whenever we visited our great-grandmother. Her language was Portuguese, and she felt we should all understand; and my dad was strong in believing that since we are in the

US, English should be spoken. My dad and his grandmother would carry on a conversation with one another; she would speak Portuguese, and he would answer in English.

Despite the number of places, I've traveled to, strangely enough, I've never been to The Azores. My global business travel never landed me there, nor has my personal travels. When I was at my height of international travel, I was too busy, and now that I'm officially retired from the company and on to other endeavors, I hope to find my way there someday. But then again, a strong work ethic is something the Portuguese are known for. And indeed, my family is no exception.

The culture reflects a talent for working together to make things happen. No doubt, a desire to achieve and a spirit of cooperation infuses everything they do. Celebrating family and community are their bedrocks, both of which were instilled in me and my siblings at a very young age.

In fact, it was both, family and community, that were at the heart of the Portuguese celebrations that we used to attend growing up. "Festas" are religious celebrations by nature, honoring Queen Isabel of Portugal (also known as "Saint Elizabeth") and her life-long dedication to the poor as she established orphanages and provided shelter to the homeless. The Festas are huge gatherings of families and friends, often numbering in the hundreds, highlighted by parades, church services, music, dancing, and plenty of food.

Wine and beer were provided for the adults and, as I remember it, an orange drink was provided for the kids and those who preferred drinking something other than alcohol. I witnessed tough, hardworking, self-guarded, people letting their guard down, appreciating others and having a great time. Those feelings of solidarity, community, and celebrating life together left a permanent impression on me as a kid.

Festas are typically held from April through June, the first week of the Pentecost traditionally mark their beginning. When we were young, we always attended the celebrations in Sacramento as well as the Festas in

Gridley, California. I distinctly remember gathering in the Portuguese hall there, then proceeding to the Church, then returning to the Portuguese hall for the celebration which always included Sopas on the menu; a traditional Portuguese dish made with meat, carrots, cabbage and spices, and simmered for hours until the spices completely infuse the broth and the meat literally falls apart. It's then generously poured into a large pan over French bread until the bread is entirely saturated.

This tradition lives on in our family today. Some may refer to Sopas as "soggy bread". I take that as a compliment, however, because as a Portuguese, I know that even the hint of a dry spot on the bread is considered a reject.

Another tradition is the Portuguese Sweet Bread. In our family traditionally baked during Easter, where an egg is placed in the center of a small amount of dough and some rolled dough over the egg symbolizing an Easter basket. More typically we would roll the dough in between our hands and tie it into a knot, for it to rise before baking. The tradition continues from my mother, then to me, then to our daughters, and now we're teaching our grandchildren.

Traditions and values, like a strong work ethic and a healthy respect for your elders served as the foundation of our home life that my parents instilled in us.

With age and my life's experiences in mind, I built upon the belief of earning my keep and, the importance of ingenuity, integrity, hard work and an appreciation of others. Life is better for all when you, "Earn your keep". https://friendsofourcommunity.com

Yuba City, California

Sutter County, California is known for its rich agricultural history. It's located in the northern part of the state, deep in the Sacramento Valley and situated along the Sacramento River which forms its western boundary. It was just outside of Yuba City where our family farm sat and where my brothers and sisters and I were born and raised. We farmed 300 (and sometimes more than 500) acres depending upon how much land my dad decided to acquire and/or rent.

Before my siblings and I were old enough to go out into the fields to provide any valuable help to dad, we spent our days with our mother who taught us the everyday tasks we would need when we went out on our own. We helped her wash dishes, clean the house, iron clothes, do the laundry, and cook. I remember her warning us, "I'm not always going to be here to take care of you. You better know how to do this stuff when you're on your own." Whenever we weren't happy about it, she'd tell us, "You will get happy in the same pants you got sad in," meaning you might be sad now, but you'll get over it soon. To this day, I'm thankful for my mother's support and foresight.

When I was five years old, my sisters and I were playing outside. They were throwing rocks, and I got in the crossfire. One of the rocks hit me in the eye and caused some hemorrhaging which blinded me for a period of time. After spending a few days in the hospital, the doctor required me to stay calm and keep my head down as my eye healed—a tall order for a five-year-old boy—so my mother taught me how to knit in order to focus my efforts. Over the course of several weeks, I knitted more than my fair share of coat hanger covers.

Our parents made sure we were involved in community activities like 4-H and the Future Farmers of America (FFA). I took cooking lessons and showed cattle at the local fair and at the Cow Palace in San Francisco as well. Music played a part in my early years too. I learned how to play the harmonica, which I still play to this day (somewhat). I wish I had something to show for the piano lessons I took. The best I can say is that I committed to memory one of those rudimentary songs for beginners which I can play till today.

When I was around seven, I ventured out into the fields to help my dad. I remember, he modified our Case tractor that we were using as a scraper to level land where we planned to build a new house. The modification consisted of adding blocks to the pedals so I could reach them. I was just thrilled to have my first job driving a tractor. Little did either of us know at that time that the little boy whose feet couldn't reach the tractor pedals would one day be director of global operations for one of the largest agriculture corporations in the world.

Out in the fields, my dad taught us, by example as well as by sayings, that I've taken with me throughout my career and personal life. He instilled in us a strong work ethic and an intolerance for laziness. Whenever he'd see a person sitting around others that were working, my dad would point him out to us saying "That guy is not afraid of work. He'll sit down right next to it." My dad would emphatically add, "Always be helpful, never be that guy."

My dad taught us how to assess, create, and deliver a plan. And in order to achieve any degree of success in life, my dad taught us to treat people fairly, to always be honest with others, to say what you mean, and do what you say, in everyday life and in every day of your life. To work alongside of him, you would be tired at the end of that day.

He taught us how to work with wood and metal, how to trouble shoot or wire a car, a truck, or a house. We learned quickly how to drive all kinds of farm equipment including tractors, forklifts, backhoes, and eighteen-wheeler trucks. We learned all about electricity, hydraulics, cutting, and welding - enabling us to modify or build our own equipment whenever we needed to.

In addition to the paddy rice we grew, the farm consisted of prune and peach trees and vegetable seed crops like watermelon, cantaloupe, squash, and cucumbers. We extracted the seeds and left the rest of the crop in the field to decay into compost. We eventually owned our own seed washer and dryer for the cucurbit crops. I remember we would come home from school and buck sacks of seed from the field to the truck. My father or one of my brothers-in-law would drive the truck to the washer, and we would transfer the sacks into bins. As I got older, I drove the truck myself and, as time went on, we adapted the equipment to place the seed directly into bins for transportation. Running the seed washer and dryer became one of my responsibilities on the farm. When the seed arrived, my dad would tell me, "We have made the crop, don't mess it up," and then left it to me to manage.

We sold our seeds to several seed companies. My dad developed a good relationship with one of the company representatives who became a good friend of the family. In the beginning, I only knew him as an older man who had a thin mustache and walked with a cane. He always came across as even-tempered, and he had an air about him that he knew what he was doing. He consistently handled business fairly. Funny how I always associated him as being a "southern gentleman" even though he didn't even have a hint of a southern accent. Anyway, his mild-mannered style reminded me of a respectful, dignified, above-board kind of gentleman.

In fact, it was he who gave me the most fundamental yet significant advice you could ever give to a seed grower: "Always pay attention to the seed." The seed's quality, he stressed, is vital. He explained the fine line between ensuring that the seeds were dried correctly and well enough, but not too much. He took the time to teach me the tricks of a seedsman: "You can get an idea of the quality of a seed lot by the way it feels in your hand, and when they crack a certain way between your teeth, you know they're dry enough."

Even though we did not always see eye to eye, me, my brothers, and my dad worked as a team, not only making sure our own work was done, but helping out each other for the greater good of the business. We each did what we needed to do on the farm; then, when that work was done, we drove the trucks hauling our products and the products of others. Not only did we drive the equipment, we maintained it as well.

In the fall of 1971, getting ready to turn eighteen in a few months, I was wondering what else I should do with my life. I considered enlisting myself in the military because, during my military examination, I scored very high on the mechanical testing. Mechanics must have been high in demand as the

Marines, and especially the Army, were requesting to meet with me. After all, my dad served in the Army and perhaps, serving in the military was just the change of scenery I needed as I wanted to see other places of the world. My lottery number was 32 and, in the opinion of the local Military Lottery office, I would likely be called in February. I was mentally prepared and proud to serve my country, but my course of action changed when President Nixon ended the draft that year. After a lot of thought, I decided to stay on the farm.

However, I did have another interest. When I graduated high school before getting into the hay business, I gave a lot of thought to becoming an auctioneer. We raised cattle, and I would see books on these big auctions, and the auctioneers that made these sales happen. There was one that I saw many times and realized that he was one of the top auctioneers. In one of these books, I saw an auctioneer school in Montana and sent for some information. Looked it over and thought, *wow*! Well, the school was far away, and I did not have the money for the tuition. This was always a dream and an alternative, but the seed business had just fully taken over my life, and then, I never looked back.

Now, this would have been sometime around 1989 as we lived in Payette, Idaho, and we were visiting Yuba City. We were staying at Lynette's parents, and they did not have an internet connection. I had some work to do and wanted a place with an internet connection. There is a Starbucks near so I went to try that. I parked my vehicle and went inside. A gentleman looked at me and asked, "From your license plate, I see that you are from Idaho. Do you know any Ranchers in the Payette area?" I told him that I was from Payette, and he stood up and held out his hand. He introduced himself and said he had done some auctions in Payette. He was the top auctioneer in the books of my past. Well, I did not mention how impressed I was to meet him, but I sat down and had a great discussion with him that led to many topics. I could not wait to tell Lynette what had happened to me that morning. I was really impressed that a person of his stature could be such a polite and humble person. I left from there hoping I could be that, to someone, someday!

With this small world example in mind here is another worth mentioning.

In the seed business we were bought and sold many times. At one point we were owned by Atlantic Richfield. I was headed to an annual meeting and my travel required a connection in Los Angles.

I arrived and then boarded the plane to Imperial, CA. I had on a coat with the company's name which was noticed by a gentleman boarding the plane and he asked if he could sit next to me.

He seemed to be interested in the Seed business. He asked me some questions and we had some pretty open an honest exchange, not agreeing on all the topics. The plane landed and we cordially said, good bye. I thought an interesting guy and he was surely interested in the seed business.

I was now in El Centro, CA and the meeting began. The president of the company addressed the group and explained the situation of our new ownership and then introduced his new boss. *Oh wow! This was the guy I sat next to on the plane. We discussed a lot of topics and some of his ideas I disagreed with - I wonder how this is going to go? I wonder if he will remember?* At the end of the meeting, we gathered and the president introduced me to Walt, his new boss.

Well, he had no idea that we already met on the plane. At that point Walt needed a ride to the hotel and I was awarded with the task as we were staying at the same hotel. *Well, at least I was provided the opportunity to spend more time with him and possibly mend some of the topics I disagreed with him on.*

However, that was not needed as he was learning and open to input so we continued our conversation over a drink at the bar. We did meet another time or two, but he was at the top of the organizational chart and I was a fieldman from Yuba City.

Now let's add 20 years to the calendar and another couple owner/transitions to the company.

My sister and her family moved to Texas, their son played soccer and became friends with one of his teammates. The two boys became close and the parents got to know each other, spent time together and eventually got together for dinner at my sister's house. During that dinner my sister was talking about her history and mentioned Yuba City, her guest then asked, "From Yuba City, would you happen to know Ron Amarel?"

My sister and brother-in-law called to tell me the story of their dinner and conversation with Walt.

My brothers, sisters, and I were well cared for by our parents. We wanted for nothing. We didn't earn any money, but at that point, we really didn't need any. Our time and efforts were for the betterment of the family farm. If any of us wanted anything, our parents were open to hear our pitch and, if we were reasonable in our request, we'd usually get what we asked for. Sometimes, however, our definition of what was reasonable varied from theirs.

Although it was a "safe" way of living, I still wanted more for myself. While I appreciated the $20 my dad would willingly give me anytime I wanted to go out on a date, I preferred to become independent and earn my own money. When I turned eighteen years old in December, many things were converging to cause me to make a very important decision: to break away from the comfort I knew and step out on my own.

I moved into a smaller house on the farm and Ron Amarel Custom Hay Business was born with a burning desire to get started a high school friend of mine, Tim, whose father worked for my dad came on board to help me in my hay business and moved into the small house with me. Tim was a hard-working guy and, like me, he was trying to find his way in life. Fortunately, my dad allowed me to use my farm pick-up for my business and that was a big help.

What made us different from all the other hay balers was that we kept our promises. As far as I was concerned, my word was my reputation, and I did everything within my power to keep my promises. I learned a lesson back then that I live by even today: Pay attention, work hard, and make few promises. But live by the promises you make. There were many hay businesses who would commit to something but not deliver on time or quality, but our commitment and client service made us stand out from the crowd.

With the help of my parents, I bought a New Holland Swather and a rake, and I consulted a friend of my dad who convinced me that the Freeman baler was the only way to go. My dad was supportive of my new endeavor as well as my desire to go out on my own. He knew that if he needed me to do something on the farm, I was always there for him, especially in the fall when the hay was completed, and the farm needed help with the harvest. At that time, I also rented thirty acres of land on which I planted alfalfa and took the crop. I would bale, store, and sell the bales to local buyers.

As my hay business was getting started, attending college was still something I wanted to pursue. In order to expand my education, I enrolled in Yuba College—the only choice for what all I had going on. Despite the understanding and cooperation, I received from my teachers, the demands of attending classes and studying, combined with the responsibility, commitment, and growth I desired for my hay business, proved to be an unworkable combination. I realized I had to choose and my hay business was successful, growing, and required my attention.

As my business grew, so did my equipment, now up to two swathers, two sets of rakes, and three balers. Dedication, hard work, and keeping my promises to my customers paid off after a short while with an agreement of two of my biggest accounts. One was for a farmer who owned around 500 acres near Beale Air Force base, up in the foothills of the Sierra Nevada's. My reputation preceded me, and he reached out with an offer to get his pasture grass hay cut and baled. When I drove out to meet him at his farm, I realized that this job was working for the son of the owner of a multi-national construction company. A good, committed, hardworking person that demanded a good job and a tight deadline. We got along well, and he became a very good account for my business.

Another lucrative account was a local farmer who owned 200 acres of newly planted alfalfa. He wanted those 200 acres baled within four nights and all the bales removed each day. This was a job I wanted and needed, but to get the job done, a harrow bed (Bale Stacker) was essential to pick up the bales and stack them at a certain location off the field. Getting this job was important to my success, but its start date and my wedding date were closer than I preferred.

My business was expanding. I expanded my equipment a short time later by investing in a hay boom and a truck to make my job easier and increase my capabilities.

I attributed it to keeping promises and delivering on time for my customers. I took notice of what I had and created the opportunity for my business to grow even more. Tim and I were very busy, but were able to keep up with the pace. I reached out to some farmers. If they'd allow me, I could come in and bale their wheat straw and remove it from their field. Their stipulation was that I complete the task in two days. It was challenging to say the least, so we had to be fast. I got the job done and, if I saw that I needed more time than what I had committed to, I made them aware of it immediately. That baled wheat straw proved to be a lucrative endeavor for my business because it was sold and delivered by a hay broker to the horse tracks in San Diego, Los Angeles, and San Francisco. The straw business grew to over 50,000 bales per year which was mostly for the race tracks, but I also filled my barn for delivery to the local feed store throughout the year.

With my growing resources of equipment, I was able to accommodate the growers' requests to remove the bales from the field the same day so they could irrigate or work the field for the next crop. By bringing my harrow bed in, I was able to remove all the bales from the field within six to eight hours. When the hay season was over, as needed, we could deliver the stacks, which gave us work into the winter. Both of my top customers wanted me to cut and bale more acres than we originally agreed to. While it was challenging, I welcomed the work because I wanted to pay off my purchased equipment. Due to the distance and travel time between home and the fields, we decided that traveling home for the night was a waste of good time. We could gain two to three hours of sleep by sleeping in the field or the pickup. I distinctly remember a time when Tim and I pushed ourselves hard for thirty-three days, then took a few days off to recuperate. With twenty-four hours in a day, we learned quickly how to make the majority of those hours as productive as possible. As my dad would tell us, "Learn how to sleep fast." Now I knew exactly what he meant.

We averaged about four to five hours of sleep each night and stayed productive for the other nineteen to twenty hours in the day. We knew a rain was predicted, and we had hay in the field, so the race began. We completed what was needed to be done and then, headed home for a few days off to recuperate. What a great feeling of success. On the way home, the rain started to fall, and it provided us with a feeling of accomplishment and comfort as well. Now, a few days of calm for us and the business.

By that time, I had been dating my girlfriend, Lynette, for a while. She was a few years younger than me, but we knew each other from high school. Our dates were far from traditional. I would pick her up, we'd have dinner sometimes, but we'd typically drive out into the fields. We'd spend time together until the dew fell; then, I would start to bale for the rest of the night while Lynette slept in the pick-up. I'd usually work all night long baling hay and when I was finished, we'd either go out to breakfast or I'd bring her home, and her mother would make breakfast for us. How I earned their trust, I'll never know. I don't think I'd be as welcoming as they were to a young guy who took one of my daughters out in the evening and didn't bring her home until 6:00 in the morning!

On Christmas Eve, 1976, I proposed marriage to her. At least, I thought I did. Lynette maintains that I merely asked her "to be mine," and did not ask her to marry me. I thought I was clear, and I thought the ring I gave her that evening would confirm it. Anyway, we were married in March of the following year.

Getting married three months after announcing our engagement may have seemed to some like a shotgun wedding. Actually, the reason we had to rush down the aisle in the month of March was because the hay season began in April, and I had to be ready to bale 200 acres for the new client. There was no way I could've done anything during the peak hay season.

Our wedding was a great celebration with family and friends. We were gratefully showered with $250 from the "money dance" which was intended for us to spend on our honeymoon. Well, we would not spend that much on our three-day honeymoon, anyway. Instead, that money went to buy baling wire and tractor fuel for my upcoming hay job. At that point, it took everything we had to prepare for the coming season. I did, however, leave $2 in our bank account just to keep it open.

Lynette moved into the house that Tim and I shared (now the three of us) and, with her nephew visiting us the during his summer vacation, Lynette settled into her new country lifestyle quite nicely.

When we were first married, I'd ask Lynette to come out for the day and drive the truck. On one particular day, she was hesitant, but I pleaded with her and said, "C'mon, I don't have anybody else today!" She agreed and we began the day's work. Lynette was driving the truck on which we had already stacked bales of hay, at least four or five layers high. I was standing on the top row as she was driving so, I could see from above what was directly ahead of us. I saw a ridge in the field. I saw it and yelled, "SLOW DOWN!!!" but it was too late. As soon as we hit the ridge, the load began to topple. I knew immediately what was coming next. Instinctively, I hurled my hay hooks in one direction so they wouldn't impale me, and I jumped off from the top of the load (about ten to twelve feet high) in the other direction, far enough so the tumbling bales wouldn't fall on me. I landed with a roll. I ran as fast as I could alongside the truck, trying to get Lynette's attention, yelling at the top of my lungs while wildly waving my arms, signaling for her to STOP!!! Lynette had no idea what happened because she was focused on what was in front of her. She only realized what had happened when she stopped the truck and got out. Needless to say, she was visibly shaken, but within some time, she was able to take it in stride.

After everything calmed down, (yes, some tenderness required) I found my hay hooks, lined up the bales, re-loaded the truck, tied down the bales and continued on for the trip to the customer. For a while afterward, Lynette vowed to never drive the truck again. Rationality and confidence returned after a short while and she was back at it, this time with some modifications. Lynette would drive the truck as long as we had a smooth field and a straight run. When she came to the end of the field, she would stop the truck and I'd come down from the load, turn the truck around, get her going straight again, and then she'd drive on until the end again. As far as I was concerned, despite the occasional interruptions—maybe two or three times per load—I was still getting the job done. As with other challenges we had to face, we found our way here as well. I know I was determined, driven, maybe a little hard-headed, and/or difficult at times. It was challenging, but the understanding, support, and love Lynette provided made me realize that I had found my soulmate for life.

Being young and in business for myself, I didn't really think about purchasing a health insurance plan as it was not so common then and very expensive. However, I wish I had insurance in December of 1978, when Lynette and I became parents for the first time. I presumed (incorrectly, it turned out) that after Lynette gave birth to our first daughter, Rebecca, I'd receive a bill from the hospital that I could pay in installments, similar to past doctor bills. Not the case as I quickly discovered. After Rebecca was born, I left the hospital that night a father, ready to begin a new chapter and role of a lifetime. I couldn't wait to get her and Lynette home to begin our new life as a family of three. The only glitch in my plan was when the hospital informed me that if I wanted to bring them home, I'd have to pay $1,500 before they were released in two days. My first question to them was what if I don't have the money? They told me in that case, they wouldn't release them and the tab would be mounting at $150 per day.

I had to think quickly and resourcefully. December is considered late in the hay season. What did I have that I could turn into an opportunity? I was in the midst of hauling with my truck as much as I could. While I normally got paid at the end of a job, I informed the farmer I was hauling for, what I was up against and asked him if he would pay me now for the work I had already completed. When he heard my dilemma, he graciously paid me for the work I had already performed for him. It was the amount I needed to pay the hospital bill.

I was still learning my new roles of being a good husband and now, a father, all the while still dedicated to carving out a name and reputation for myself in my hay business. Winter was here and hay season was over. I was in my father's shop working on equipment when I received a call from the president of a vegetable seed company, informing me that they were looking for a person to help them in the Northern California region. A person who could help complete their contracting with growers for the next year, and he asked me if I would be interested. He knew I had seed production experience due to working with dad and running my dad's seed dryer. When he made me an offer, my first thought was that I was too busy to accept more work. After all, I recently quit college to focus on my hay business. Why would I want yet another job? I politely told him I'd think it over, and if I could find someone who could fit their bill, I'd let them know.

After talking it over with Lynette, I realized that even with a bustling hay business, there were off-season periods when I didn't earn any income. The seed company would pay me each month consistently. I called the president back and provided my proposal, "I keep my hay and farming business but I will help you out the best I can." Without much effort on either side, it was agreed upon and in January of 1979, I became a fieldman, responsible for their Northern California production of onion and cucurbit crops.

I came to understand quickly the saying, "Be careful what you wish for." Working for the company during the day and working at my hay business at night, I had to put myself on an uncompromising schedule. I'd put a full day's work in at the seed company and bale hay all night. A typical day brought me home at 2:00 a.m. and get up at 6:00 a.m. ready to put in another full day's work in the field and at the office, which was a desk in our laundry room. With a good relationship and understanding of the seed company, we made it work, and they were happy.

When I found out later that year that the company was being sold, I was relieved to a certain point. I figured it was a good ride while it lasted. I really wasn't thrilled about working for a big company, and I had a lot of work calling my name in the hay business. And anyway, I was literally exhausted from the schedule I put myself on. But then again, things have a funny way of changing. When I found out that the new company wanted to keep me, I was stunned. With our second child on the way, I did an about-face when their offer included health insurance coverage. I remembered the predicament I was in when our first daughter was born and now, with a second one on the way, it was an offer I simply couldn't ignore. Even though I was much better prepared than before, this was an offer I could not refuse. They offered me a promotion to Northern California, Production Manager with the stipulation that I get out of my hay business. I accepted their offer with a planned phase out time. Tim and I, as a team, now had more to do. We both worked full steam ahead covering the needs of both jobs. We did not see it as the hay business and the seed business; we saw it as our job and dealt with the priorities of both which we managed as one. But with my responsibilities growing at the seed company, letting the hay business go was easier to accept. But what about Tim? I did not want to leave a dedicated person like him, high and dry, so with some negotiation I was able to get him hired on with the seed company. Wow, the same dedicated team, him and I, on to another endeavor. I found a local guy who wanted to expand his own hay business so, I suggested that he lease my equipment and take over my customers. By the second year my phase-out plan was working in my favor.

Our second daughter Terra was born in December of 1980. Needless to say, Lynette and I were thrilled! We were a family of four now and discussed how we saw our future. We decided that four children were the most we wanted. Our plan was that if our third child was a boy, we'd stop there. But if our third child was a girl, we'd have another child. That was our plan, no more than four.

In the meantime, the company was looking for land to enlarge its operations. They wanted to build an office and a shop, as well as some green houses to conduct their tomato research in Yuba City. The solution was right before our eyes. My dad partitioned off three acres of his farm for this expansion plan. In fact, my former hay shed became a warehouse for the company.

Things were going well. The company was expanding, and so was our family. When we found out that Lynette was pregnant again, our strategic family planning was essentially planned for us. In January of 1983, our twin girls, Carrie and Ashlie, were born, blessing us with four beautiful daughters. As previously agreed, our family was now complete.

Work and family responsibilities were going along smoothly. I was deep into the seed business and out of the hay business. I decided that since my evenings were free, this would be the perfect time to return to Yuba College enrolling in their night school. Together with a good friend and colleague Gary, I went back to complete my studies. I was working during the day and going to school at night, and Lynette was running a day care in our home that helped. By June of 1987, I graduated Yuba College.

Another change in the company ownership brought further change as their first strategic business decisions was to close the operations in Yuba City and reduce to one fieldman in the area. At that time, I was offered the position of Pacific Northwest Regional Manager, an opportunity and an interesting position, but it would require a move to Idaho.

Relocating to another state would mean uprooting my wife and four daughters and losing the support of both sides of our family. On the other hand, the farm was clearly not big enough to sustain four families; my parents, my brothers and I. If I stayed on the farm, we had to expand and increase the family business.

I had options and a great opportunity in front of me with this new position asking for more responsibilities than I ever had. We knew this move would be a big change in our lives. However, I will continue to work to someday become the head of production of the company. After weighing the pros and cons of staying on the farm, considering what was best for my family and others, we decided it was best to make the move to Idaho.

My dad was not very thrilled when I told him. Naturally, the farm was his dream, and my leaving was not in his plan. My dad was emphatic when he told me he thought I was making a big mistake. When he realized that my mind was made up, he agreed. I should to go my own way. It was clear that he was not happy and unintentionally, I knew I hurt him, but I had to do what I thought was best.

I had four growing children and a wife whose lives I was about to disrupt. I was leaving behind the support of our families. I had no hay business left. And now, I had basically burned the bridge of ever returning to work on our family farm. Working through the comments of others and my own emotions together with Lynette, we decided to move to Idaho. As we drove off, leaving our home town with a feeling of excitement, fighting off the emotions of leaving our parents, I asked God to help us. "I've got to take care of these five ladies—that's the job you gave me. With your help, I will do it well. I'm heading for Idaho, and if You can find a way to provide for us, I will somehow do my best to repay You."

Payette, Idaho

It was December of 1987 when my family and I moved to Idaho. When we arrived, I remember seeing a T-shirt with the image of Sylvester the Cat on it that said, "Welcome to Boithiee! Set your clock back twenty years!" From what I know now, I don't think Sylvester is quite accurate about the twenty years, but I can say that living in Idaho does bring you back to a more wholesome way of life. And while at the time, I did not have a clue what to expect, I can say that we felt genuinely welcomed with open arms into the heart of Payette, our new hometown.

Its environment and offerings suited our family well. It stirred a feeling in our hearts that made us happy to call it home for what would be the next four years of our life.

It started with the relaxed and friendly conversation I had with the owner of Teele's Hardware Store, located on Main Street in Downtown Payette, who immediately knew we were new in the neighborhood. "So, you guys are new in town," he stated. I told him about the green and white house on 2nd Avenue South that we'd bought, and that we needed keys for the internal doors. The bedrooms had locks, but we did not have keys. He knew exactly what house we were talking about. Just having made our acquaintance, he entrusted me with three or four skeleton keys to take back to our house. He commented, "It is one or two of these. Keep the ones that work and bring back the ones that don't; they are a dollar each."

The hospitality of the town continued with the friendships we built with the parents of our daughters' new school friends and friends made from the church we attended nearby. People welcomed our children into the neighborhood as if they were their own. A local farming couple with children that matched our family well, became friends.

Here, in Payette, people cared about each other. When we saw the effect of living here on our daughters; Lynette and I realized these were our kind of people.

We witnessed this facet again in the ease with which the sister from our new church visited our home and really made us all feel welcome. I'll always remember the party we catered for her as she celebrated her twenty-fifth year in the convent. We promised to provide barbecue chicken, beans and salad for her celebration. That Saturday afternoon, we were prepared to serve anywhere from 100 to 150 people for the party, serving lunch from 2:00 p.m. Sister literally panicked when we pulled into the church parking lot at 9:00 a.m. that morning in a nonchalant manner; she expected us to have arrived earlier for what we had promised to deliver. While I told her not to worry, and that we had it all under control, my assurances didn't seem to calm her. The only thing I could tell her at that point was, "I'll do what I need to do," and asked her to please pray for our success. When 2:00 p.m. rolled around, things went off flawlessly like clockwork. The food was ready, people were being served, and everyone was happily celebrating the sister's years of service. We enjoyed the event and met a lot of good people. When the sister came to me, amazed at the results, I told her that it was her prayers that made it all possible.

There was also a splendid, pristine spot we found on the lake that we returned to at every chance we got. It was the spot where our daughters learned to fish, swim, and water ski. Our grandchildren are now learning water sports at the same location their mothers learned.

At that point in our lives, we wanted a place for our family to be happy and safe, and it was clear that we found everything we were looking for in Payette.

Being a regional manager, my job responsibilities included routine travel throughout the Pacific Northwest which included the states of Idaho,

Oregon, and Washington. I got to see the beauty of the Pacific Northwest. For all intents and purposes, everything was going well.

However, in the fall of 1989, we had a bad year. The seed company was in financial trouble and a restructure was required. The company did its best to implement a plan for restructuring, creating a plan to provide the best outcome for our suppliers and growers. As a regional manager, it was my responsibility to implement the plan in my area.

As the negative rumors about the Company began to swirl, I realized, something needed to be done. I put together a communication plan which included a couple of face-to-face meetings with our growers and suppliers. I really felt that the rumors and the perception was much worse than the actual facts, and this was not a time for the company to hide but to confront its issues straight forward with honesty. Oh, we were struggling—no doubt—but the one thing that kept ringing true for me was the Company had to communicate its situation and its plan. We had to be transparent with our employees our suppliers, and growers. If that meant standing up in front of them and taking our hits, then that's what we absolutely had to do.

I discussed my communication plan with the president of the company, and he agreed to support me. He would provide me the details that I could communicate at the meetings. I greatly appreciated his commitment and support.

Fortunately, we had a strong core group of individuals who shared a strong commitment to the company. I can truly say that we wouldn't have made it without them. Together, we supported the company and each other through open and frequent communication.

I reached back into my hay business days that taught me all about commitment, and promises, and delivering on them. I believed it called upon the same skills of commitment—delivering with honesty, transparency, and maintaining promises.

I held the first of several meetings at a hotel in Nampa, Idaho, to accommodate the multitude of growers, customers and suppliers. One of the company's fieldmen was standing there with me. There we were, standing in front of a bunch of unhappy people. I was warned I'd be walking into a lion's den; it was very likely that an ambush awaited me, but my commitment was strong that I knew I was doing the right thing. I convinced myself that I would have appreciated someone doing this for me if I was in their place. And, by the way, I used to be one of them.

Leaving the growers and everyone else high and dry was not an option. If we could be transparent with people, the power of communication and commitment would provide the foundation and understanding in support of the Company and its future. With a strong will and wobbling knees, at the thought of my reception, I faced the crowd.

I told them everything I knew and to keep my promise of transparency, I said some things they did not want to hear too. Right off the bat, it was the wives of the growers who really let me have it. Fingers waving and voices raised, I was called a lot of things that evening. They called me out for collecting a paycheck when they weren't receiving one. They emphatically pointed out that my life was going to go on without an interruption. They heard my words but they wanted to be paid. I told them that I understood what I had to tell them wasn't enough; I promised to hold another meeting to provide them more information. I asked them for their cooperation and told them I'd do my best to come back in two weeks with as many answers as I could.

I took those "hits" because I couldn't counter their pain with some boilerplate phrases, void of empathy and compassion. They were rightfully angry, and I knew it. Honesty and transparency were my only arsenal in this situation, and I called upon both as I addressed the crowd and their accusations. I, like they, were part of this situation, trying to find a solution. I knew I had to manage the personal comments and insults, then respond with professionalism and sympathy—knowing I would act the same if I were in their shoes.

I stayed after the meeting to allow those who wanted to address me individually to do so. If words were knives, I would have not survived. Then, one of our bigger growers approached me. He acknowledged that while I had gone through a lot that evening, and he did not like what I was putting them through, he appreciated me being there to address the group. At that point, I realized I had done the right thing.

It was over, and I was sure that Lynette would be wondering how it went, so it was good to get home and discuss it with her. However, it was hard to explain without a quivering voice and emotions.

I held a similar meeting in Central Oregon at a local restaurant. One grower in particular asked me if I planned to stay with the company, and if so, would I promise him that I would stay?

My mind was racing; I only made promises that I knew I could keep. For this particular gentleman who stood in front of me, I couldn't promise him that I'd stay with the company because the company could terminate me at any point in time. Instead, what I promised him was that I wouldn't quit the company. At least, I felt I was in control of that.

I explained everything to them, and afterward, the same grower impatiently asked me if I was finished talking. I figured he was just going through the motions and wanted me to shut up so he could leave. Instead, he said, "I am busy with many things to do; just tell me what you want me to grow and give me the contract because I'm ready to sign it." In the end, we signed one hundred percent of the growers which was key to the success of the company, enabling the company to produce the seed needed for the forecasted sales, that made it possible for our growers and suppliers to receive a high percent of what was owed to them in a reasonable amount of time.

After I gained their trust and they realized I was doing my best on their behalf, they found me more approachable. Our interaction became more normal, meaningful, and productive which came as a great relief.

It taught me that while literally standing up in front of people and taking your hits may be a tough deal, you have to do what is honorable and fair to others. Armed with transparency and a sincere desire to find a solution for the betterment of the situation as a whole is enough of a "shield" to protect against any insult or accusation hurled your way. This was a case of perceptions (the unknown) being worse than reality and a good lesson that I learned.

When people put their trust in you, no matter personal or professional, you have to do everything in your power to respectfully return the trust and dedication they provided.

If you stay the course of strength, trueness, and integrity, people will listen to you. Strength that comes from believing in your cause and striving with all your efforts to do what's right. It's human nature to gravitate to the truth and strength. If you're transparent, fair, supportive, and truthful with people, they will normally come toward you.

The company survived because of the committed, passionate employees who remained strong and willing—together with a lot of understanding, hardworking, and dedicated growers. *Wow, what an experience.*

The planned restructure provided me another opportunity which would send me back to California to be in the main office as the Head of Global Seed Production. After only four years in Payette, Hollister, California was now going to be our new home. While I knew it was going to be a good move for me professionally, my family's preference was to stay in Payette.

Hollister, California

We were moving to Hollister with mixed emotions. When I say "we," I mean me. My family's emotions weren't mixed at all. They wanted to remain in

Payette. I was achieving my "stretch goal" of becoming the Head of Global Seed Production and Processing, with it, I was about to embark on the most extensive international travel schedule I could ever imagine to the company's various seed production locations that included China, Inner Mongolia, Thailand, Vietnam, India, South Africa, Europe, Chile, Argentina, and Peru.

I needed to be in Hollister, CA coming from Idaho, and the new head of sales needed to be in Hollister coming from Arizona. He already had an apartment, and we agreed that the two of us would live together in a two-bedroom apartment until we could arrange the move of our families. I was traveling international, and he was traveling in the US, so we did not meet too often, but we became close friends. He was able to find a home, and it was ready to move into. I was in China and would return in ten days. He informed me that he was moving into his house and would cancel the apartment. *Whoa, this is too fast. Where do I go if the apartment is canceled?* He informed me that we would live together in his new home and that all my stuff was already moved. We both lived out of our suitcase, so that was maybe a few hangers of shirts. When I returned, he would be in Florida, so the directions to the new home and a key were on my desk at the office. I arrived back from China late that night, went to the office, got the key, and left to find this new house in the dark. I arrived at the place. The key worked; I went to the room he described in the note, found my stuff, found the shower, and crawled into bed. For some, this may be strange, but we have lived together before, and we are both used to bedding down in a new location while traveling. Later, his wife showed up, and it was the three of us until I could find another place.

The president of the company was living in an apartment with the VP of finance, but the VP found a home for himself, so there was a place in the apartment with the president. I moved in there until I could find my own apartment.

Before Lynette and the girls joined me in Hollister, I lived with three other employees in four different places. I was trying to create a routine for myself and wanted to remain committed to staying in shape. I joined a local gym and it fit the bill perfectly. I became friends with my new work-out buddies, John and Jim, very soon. Their appearances wouldn't have earned them any fashion awards; therefore, we had a lot in common. Open, honest, and talented gentlemen they were for sure. (I invited them both to a barbecue I was hosting at our home. As I looked over at my driveway, I commented to John, "Hey, somebody just drove up to my house in a Jaguar." "Oh! That's Jimmy!" he exclaimed. Jim has left us now, but will always be remembered for his soft-spoken advice in a style of his own. John and I continue to enjoy our friendship as we share and challenge our life experiences.

Our daughters had to face a change of school and the loss of friends. It was a tough move for each of them. They all missed Idaho, especially Rebecca. Although we were only in Idaho for four years, we all liked Idaho and were happy to call it home.

After Rebecca entered high school, she made a commitment of her own and stated that I had four years to get back to Idaho. If we were not back by then, she would return on her own to attend college at Boise State. (Apparently, Rebecca takes the same stand as I do on making promises because she enrolled in Boise State after graduating high school, built her career, and she and her husband continue to raise their family in Idaho.).

My schedule was set according to the crop processes, and the various growth stages of the crops. I was always in contact with the local company personnel to inform me when I should see the crops and then, structure my schedule accordingly. I tried to take to heart the words of wisdom my work-out buddy Jim always told me, "Slow down and relax. Don't get too high strung about things." He was obviously speaking from experience but my reality had not yet reached that point. It was good advice; however, one that I'd be keeping in the back of my mind.

I was going to be traveling up to seventy percent of the time now. It's one thing to fly hours into a major international city. It's quite another to then travel up to eight hours through the countryside to the fields where the work really began. Keeping my tasks and schedule in order required talented and continued support. I was blessed with talented, dedicated assistants that worked harder than I. Basically, in the forty-two years of my career, I had two assistants. They were the best and greatly appreciated. Call it coincidence or fate – the three of us shared the same birthday.

In fact, thinking of their dedication, I am reminded of the times the company was selling, and we had to entertain many potential buyers. Sometimes, it was a presentation in the morning and another that afternoon. As I remember, there was a time we did five presentations in one week. We had listened to each other's presentation so many times that we could have switched off. To keep it interesting, one of my colleague's made a bet with me that he could give his presentation in a shorter time than I. If nothing else, this made us both more efficient. During one of the presentation's, I was the clear winner, giving my presentation is a shorter time, and then he asked me a question of his own that he knew would take me time to explain. Cheater! The bet was the winner buys the other a beer that he still owes me today.

SOWING

"Remember this: Whoever sows sparingly will also reap sparingly,
and whoever sows generously will also reap generously."

— 2 CORINTHIANS 9:6

"We know we cannot plant seeds with closed
fists. To sow, we must open our hands."

— ADOLFO PÉREZ ESQUIVEL

Management Style

The symbolic meaning of an open hand has existed in various forms for thousands of years—as a gesture of peaceful intentions toward another, or as a symbol of good faith when making an oath or promise. I've always strived to greet people with an open hand as I know, 'seed is never sown with a closed hand.'

By the time I reached Hollister, California to assume my role as VP of Operations, I was doing my best to develop a management style that I could build on. I had a lot to learn, and I knew I needed to earn my respect. It wasn't something I was automatically given, nor automatically entitled to. I also knew that in order to be successful, I had to rely on others. I had to be rigid in my style and beliefs, but flexible enough to change course mid-stream, if need be, in order to succeed. It was clear to me – the job is bigger than me, and I had to rely on others. Management training was something I needed, and when provided, enjoyed.

Many times, I had to stop and admit that I did not understand everything I needed to know about a subject. I realized that the best option is to rely on others that are more knowledgeable and talented than I am. I would do my research, listen to, and ask others to be part of the solution with responsibility and autonomy included. I found this as a key element in correctly identifying the scope and increasing the efficiency and results. In the process, I would tell others in the company my opinion bluntly, especially if I'd disagree, in order to prompt them to open up with their opinion, knowing that I need more time to think, gather more information, and sort things out. I was probably not alone on this, but patience was not my virtue. I may have forcefully provided my opinion prior to my thoughtful conclusion, but that is something I try to manage now, avoiding a needful apology. I try, but I drive forward with honesty and my open opinions, at times, still prevail. Some decisions have to be made alone, but I prefer to gather the facts and opinion of others and then decide. Once we decide on a plan and it is in place, I expect all involved to be on board, knowing the importance of keeping them on the path and engaged.

One thing I learned from my father: "Do not ask anyone to do anything that you would not do yourself." It was with this approach that I began my new role.

I was also ready to begin my new responsibilities on an international level, hoping that my talent and skills provide me the ability to relate with foreigners efficiently and effectively. I kept reminding myself that seed is never sown with a closed fist.

It is wonderful how the lessons you learn early on really do serve as the template for your actions later in life, when the stakes are higher and your responsibilities are greater.

As VP of Operations, my lessons in integrity and moral values were tested. I built a resistance early on to never allow anyone to compromise either of them. Challenge them, fine. But change them, absolutely not.

I clearly remember we were behind on our numbers and the year end was approaching quickly. If we could only sell enough of this one particular carrot variety, we would be really close to reaching our numbers. The problem was that I had this particular variety on a quality hold which meant I wouldn't be able to release it to sales. I was asked to release the quality hold on the crop by the end of the day so we could include it in the sales figures. Feeling the pressure and sensing the need, I explained my concerns, but agreed to carefully review the possibilities again. Even though we were still awaiting the final test results on the crop itself, from the information I did have, I came to the same conclusion that it was too risky to release that carrot crop.

It wasn't just my integrity that was on the line; it was the integrity of others as well as the company. Sure, we may make the numbers but at the cost of complaints and recalls that may jeopardize the numbers anyway.

At the end of the day, my boss came into my Hollister office and asked if I released the crop. When I told him I hadn't, he informed me in no uncertain terms that I was insubordinate, and he had no other choice but to fire me. When I tried to reason with him, he told me I was fired and I was asked to leave the company right then and there.

After his explosion, he left for the evening. I stayed late to see what else, if anything, I could do to make the numbers. On a wing and a prayer, I tried to find a way to still reach our goal without releasing the crop. I started the process of putting other crops and priorities into place. The next morning, I got to work exceptionally early to review my plan and strategy with the people involved. We found that it was not only possible, but with a few minor adjustments, doable.

As I was diligently working toward our new goal with people in Oregon and Idaho, my boss walked into my office and demanded to know why I was still there after he fired me the day before. I told him what my plan was and if he wanted to make the numbers without jeopardizing the company's reputation, he was going to need me. He became enraged, and informed me that I, not him, would be held responsible if the numbers were not met, and he would be even more determined to see that I was ousted—this time for good.

My gut reaction got the better of me and, without much consideration for my tone, I told him, "It's your choice to throw me in with the sharks, but I know how to swim, and I will survive." His parting words to me were, "I'll leave you alone, and we will see."

The final results of the crop confirmed my quality hold, but the alternative plan provided the expected results. I double checked with everyone who worked with me to implement the plan, and they confirmed that the numbers were in the bag. I stood my ground on not releasing the crop, working together with the team to reach the desired result for the company. I was most grateful for the cooperation and support of those around me as we worked together to make the plan a success.

I walked into my boss's office and informed him of the results. He insisted on checking the numbers out himself before conceding the point. He later came to my office and thanked me for my hard work and effort to implement my plan and see it through to its successful end. Strange how things work, but we were able to put this incident behind us as we, later, not only worked together on solving other issues, but lived and traveled together as well. His assistant at that time, who I knew well, was aware of all of this—a memory we share with amazement and some humor. *The day I was fired and did not leave.*

Seedsmen often travel to the same areas, for the same reasons, and at the same times. Our schedules revolve around critical crop stages that dictate the where, why, and when of our careers. I've boarded many planes in other countries, even in the far reaches of the Earth, only to greet a handful of fieldmen from other companies. They're always reliable for a great story and a good recommendation for the best inexpensive hotel in the area. However, accommodations do not always work out, and you have to deal with what you get.

When traveling in the northern region of Asia the local hotel was closed without our knowledge. There was no place to stay, but this would not be the first time I'd slept in a vehicle. An alternative was found, so the local manager and I spent the night in a Northern Asia coal mine bunkhouse.

International travel has its own inherent difficulties. Not only do language barriers exist, but your approach to their culture is important. Most places we travel to, the people there speak English pretty well. That makes our communication so much easier, but care needs to be taken. I have found that many understand the words you are saying but the translation in their head may not correlate with your meaning or intent. This misunderstanding can happen in both directions. As details are important to the success of any project, making sure you have an accurate understanding and alignment is important. Experience taught me that, in a lot of cases, I was the problem.

When in a foreign country, I value their culture. Even though I would respectfully challenge my local colleagues, I hope they valued my presence as much I did theirs. I really enjoyed the times, having dinner with them and their families (something I may have not thanked them enough for). In turn, my family has met many of them, either in the field or at our own dinner table. To me, any colleague from out of the area should never eat alone. Our dinner table has hosted colleagues and seed company officials from many countries of the world.

In this high-tech, high-quality, dynamic business, you will encounter production issues at some point in your career. The number of variables that affect seed production is many, and on some, we have no control. That is why it is important to control everything possible. I call this "Control the Controllables."

With the challenges of seed production in mind, here are a few experiences and learning points I recall.

First experience – A company was scheduled to specifically address the issues between their and our companies. Therefore, I brought myself up to speed.

After we initially presented our solution points the negotiations began. There was a lot of attitude and rigidity from both sides. It didn't take long for me to see that we were at a clear disadvantage. Their team knew everything we were saying, yet, without a translator on our side, we couldn't understand a word of what they were saying, other than what the translator supplied, and he was one of them.

I abruptly asked for a break and summoned a colleague into our meeting to balance our communication gap. It was interesting to see the shift in the tone of the meeting and the added thought before speaking out from their side. Although we made some progress, they held strong to their position and while we were willing to give, we weren't willing to give in.

In light of our options, we made a final proposal, one that I wasn't thrilled with. The agreement was more complicated than I had wanted it to be, but allowing them to leave without an agreement was not an option. We made an agreement with some conditions.

I informed them that I would uphold our side of the agreement, but I would be traveling to their company and visit their fields next year to hold them accountable for their side of the bargain. Again, I wanted to assure that our agreement was not misunderstood and correctly implemented. I did travel there to follow up on the agreement in the fields first hand.

It was during the one-on-one visits, however, that we learned to honor our respective professional positions and, even more, realized we had more in common than we thought. In fact, we built a relationship that led us to a future joint venture. It was a win-win that we both saw as capitalizing on a problem.

Second experience – Unfortunately, a situation can escalate to the point of hiring lawyers to prepare for court or arbitration hearing. In foreign countries, understanding the legalities can get complicated. The US lawyers hired local counsel to assist us with the nuances and procedures of the local laws.

Negotiating with the local manager of the company—a gentleman that I traveled with and knew well—was not an easy task. Personal relationship aside, this was a business matter, a crucial one at that, and we were both vehemently supporting our respective company's case. Before I left the US, I knew our plan, and our limits. I arrived there with our US attorneys to begin the negotiations.

With the arbitration date looming in front of us, there were a lot of heated discussions between the lawyers on both sides. It was clear we weren't making any substantial progress in this way. I asked to be able to speak with the local manager directly, without any interference or intermediary. Naturally, our attorneys argued against my idea but, with perseverance, I got my way and made a call to the local manager

We each had negotiation points and limits. With the arbitration scheduled for the next day, a deal between us didn't look promising at all. We ended our call by agreeing to meet in person, prior to the arbitration, for a one-on-one discussion, despite the opinion of the attorneys. Given the volatile nature of our previous discussions and all that lay on the line for each company, we agreed that one lawyer from each side could join us, for observation only, and the negotiations would be left to the two of us.

Our conversations became heated as we pushed each other's limits, representing our point of view in protecting the position of our company. Going to the outer limits of our authorities, we found ourselves at a standstill. After a short break to re-group, we listened to advice from our attorneys, and confirmed our position to keep the supplier producing for us and to work within the agreed limits. I came back with my best and final proposal. It was given some consideration but ultimately, it was rejected, which led to yet another heated discussion. It appeared that the arbitration will be needed as we were both not able to agree.

After a rather lengthy break, I was approached with a change. At this point, I was outside of my limits, but I could include a benefit for future productions. Although our new terms led to even more heated discussions, we eventually came to an agreement. With the arbitration hearing starting within an hour, we decided to take our agreement to the arbiters.

We reduced our verbal agreement to writing and presented it to the arbitration panel. The arbiters asked us some questions, with a couple of our responses being challenged by the arbiters. After defending our respective positions, the arbiters ultimately approved our agreement and it was recorded. We congratulated each other. We were done, relieved, and exhausted and began to walk out of the room with our attorneys. As we were leaving the room, the local manager turned to me and asked if we were still in town this evening. When I said, "Yes," he said, "In that case, how about we do dinner together?" I asked him to pick a nice restaurant.

The attorneys were blown away. They couldn't believe that after all the fighting and arguing, we would want to enjoy a nice dinner together. They had a difficult time understanding that we both liked and respected each other, but this was business and hence, had to be dealt with differently. We had to defend our respective positions, and we both diligently did so. Even though there was a point wherein we wanted to kill each other to win for our company, we could move on after it was over. We didn't let that get in the way of our mutual respect for each other and could move on.

This experience confirmed for me that business decisions can be separate from personal feelings as long as there is a willingness and understanding on both sides. We were both dedicated and strong-willed employees who would do whatever possible to defend our company and our positions, but our personal feelings of respect for each other remained.

If a balance of business and personal ethics is maintained and respected, then moral values and friendships are not compromised. With this person in mind - Here is how I see it; "If you challenge my business or my position, I will fight with all my might against you. If it is not business and is personal, I will fight for you."

Third Experience - When our company purchased another vegetable seed company in the middle east, I was tasked with assessing our new business and location. When I arrived, I met with the head of production and manager there and started to evaluate the issues we were facing.

After meeting individually with all of the employees to discuss their concerns and opinions, I developed a transition plan which I presented to a couple of the employees for their input. With their input, some modifications were made. With close advice and agreement with them, we agreed to proceed with the newly developed plan.

I called the company president in the US and told him about my plan. He was in agreement, commenting that I stay as long as needed to ensure my plan is implemented properly.

The elephant in the room, so to speak, was one of the managers. His job was going to be eliminated. The only burning question remaining wasn't exactly how we would tell him. It was who would tell him. The former owners of the company forewarned me of making this decision. They expressed their concern and made me aware of the gun behind his desk. I was told in no uncertain terms that if I wanted him gone, I'd have to do it myself. Staying to the plan, I told them I would let him go the next day. They pressed me for a time when I'd be telling him, and I replied, "At 9:00 a.m." They told me that they'd be coming into work at noon the next day.

The next day, I went to his office where he invited me to sit down, and we began to talk. I couldn't help but notice the imposing rifle leaning up against the wall in the corner. *Something to pay attention to.* He knew something was up. I proceeded to explain the situation to him from my point of view. I informed him of the challenges I had, and told him that, according to the plan, he would be let go.

He leaned forward across his desk and, looking me directly in the eye, asked, "So, you're basically telling me that I don't have a job anymore?" I stayed calm, remained grounded in the truth, continued looking him in the eye and said, "Yes, that's basically it." I explained the plan in more detail. He stood up, leaned forward and said, "I am tired of people playing with me. I knew this was coming, but I appreciate you coming to me directly and with honesty. If you agree to listen to my issues," he continued, "I will cooperate with you." I told him that I would listen and help him in any way I could. At this point, I thought it would be a good idea to bring up the gun and inform him that having guns in the work place was not according to company rules and that he should consider leaving it home. Before I knew it, he grabbed the rifle. I had no idea what he was going to do next. To my shock and surprise, he flipped the rifle around and handed it to me with the barrel turned toward him. I accepted it from his hands, held onto it for what seemed an eternal couple of seconds, and then, respectfully handed it back to him with the barrel facing me. He took the rifle and carefully placed it back against the corner wall.

In that instant, I witnessed an expression of trust. Hard to explain as I do not know what really happened emotionally here, but this non-verbal exchange that had just taken place cemented a bond between us that we both seemed to feel. *Wow, sometimes things happen so fast and that could have so easily led to a different outcome with an overreaction from one side or the other.*

I then listened as he expressed his issues and concerns. I was totally transparent with him, honestly desiring to make this transition for him as smooth and solid as I could. We were able to come to some agreements while other issues needed more consideration. I promised to get back to him as soon as I could. That night, I was able to obtain more information from the US office to address his issues. So, the next afternoon, I made an appointment to meet with him once more. I entered his office with some confidence but more nervous than the first time. I informed him of the new information gained over night. He then informed me that he may not agree with everything I mentioned, but he appreciated the communication and looked forward to discussing it further. Then he added, "By the way, I took my gun home." *Now that was good to know.*

Seed production takes you mainly to the rural areas of many countries. We are fortunate to visit these great areas of the world as part of our job. It is not easy work, but you are exposed to beautiful terrains and wonderful, very hospitable people.

Traveling to these areas required a lot of road time, and I can remember three occasions requiring special attention. Two especially, as we were escorted by armed military personnel and vehicles. When I think back on this, I remember what I told my girls, "Respect the power of a seed." Some trips were quieter and others were full of conversations. Normally, a 'how are you,' 'how are the crops,' 'what are the problems,' 'how we can improve,' and then, it can stray to politics, hobbies, religion, and culture. As known, if you want to know someone, travel with them.

Another incident that got my attention was while I was traveling in India. It was a long day in the fields after which, we returned to the city. The local Manager and I would check in the hotel, and then, go to dinner. I received my key and entered the elevator to get to my room and get ready for dinner. The elevator reached the correct floor and the door opened. Three men rushed, and I heard some clicking and clucking. The one man standing in front of me asked me to step forward off of the elevator. I did as he said, as he had a rifle pointed at my head. One man on his right and another on his left with rifles pointed at me as well. The words began.

He asked, "Why are you on this floor?"

I replied, "I was given this floor, but maybe, I made a mistake."

He asked, "Do you have your key?"

I replied, "It is in my pocket, and if it is okay, I will slowly reach in my pocket to show you."

He replied, "Go ahead."

I asked, "Before I do so, do the other two men understand what I am doing?"

He replied, "Do as we agreed, now."

I slowly put down my briefcase and reached into my pocket and handed him the key. He asked for my passport and that was also provided in a slow and cautious way. I was informed to stand straight and not move as he walked over and made a call. He then handed me the key and my passport and informed me to continue to my room, down the hall and to the right. I gathered my things and headed for the room. I entered the room with a racing heart and then thought, *I should feel good as the security is great here. This has never happened to me before, and I'm not sure what to think.* I washed up and headed back to the elevator with care. They were all still there and the main guy told me, "Have a nice evening." When I got to the front desk, I asked the executive, "What is going on?" He apologized and said that he did not mean to put me on that floor as there was extra security due to some governmental officials staying on that floor. Once I was known, checked, and approved, all was okay.

Ok, moving on now. As with every seed company, South America is an important seed production area. Chile was a major off-season production location for us so I traveled there often. The local company we worked with there, we later purchased, and we were looking to fill the local manager's position. It was ultimately decided that we would manage the company from the US. I was asked to develop a plan to support this decision and was offered the chance to move to Santiago. Although I felt it would be a great opportunity, my family thought otherwise. As a result, it was agreed that I would spend more time there until a new manager was hired, and the implementation plan was fully executed.

For a year, one of my coworkers and I took turns managing the Chile operations; the plan was for each of us to alternate spending three weeks in Chile and then returning to the US for two weeks, and then begin that cycle again. This would provide for a one-week overlap. I welcomed that opportunity to become more immersed in the Chilean culture—a place I have visited many times and enjoyed.

We lived in a small house situated on a farm north of Santiago. The Chilean capital city was close enough for us to do our usual Sunday shopping there, stocking up on provisions for the week ahead. It was nice to be together when our visits overlapped, but for the most part, we were each on our own. Our small digs (Casa de Gringos) consisted of a couple beds, a nice bathroom, and a kitchen. Really pretty good for a farm house in the countryside of Chile.

Being away from our family for extended periods of time is never easy, but not new to either of us. Luckily, we both have understanding spouses and children that allowed us to make the most of our careers.

Chile is an absolutely beautiful country, and the employees at the company were very helpful and hospitable to us. They invited us to their homes to have dinner with them and their families. I'll always remember those meals and their gracious hospitality.

Together, we were visiting one of the production areas south of Santiago. One of our colleagues from Holland was to meet us there. We all visited the production fields and then, would return to Santiago to fly back home for the holidays. Our Dutch colleague remained in the production area to see more crops. Me and my US coworker left Santiago that night unaware of the earthquake that hit the production area we just left. When we landed in Florida early the next morning, we discovered that there had been a huge earthquake south of Santiago. Our Dutch colleague who was scheduled to fly back to the Netherlands after his field visits was caught in the quake, but he was okay. Being in the southern region with rivers in between there and Santiago. His return to Santiago became difficult. With a couple bridges collapsed, the highway was closed. With the help of the local employees, our Dutch colleague made it back to Santiago. At one point, he had to literally walk across the river with his suitcase held over his head to meet his colleagues on the other side. We did our best to manage and monitored his travel to assure he arrived back home safely. Our travels take us to many places in the world, and this is an example of our commitment to take care of one another.

There are other examples of mistakes and incidences that required local and global approaches to address the issues at hand, but we always knew that the local employees and the company had our backs.

I experienced something while I was on a trip to Asia in the year 2000. I was in Inner Mongolia visiting the crops there and then, the Gobi Desert to continue to Hong Kong, and would enter southern China from there, and then, on to Vietnam, and Thailand. My travels were going well, and I was at the end of the second week when I arrived in Hong Kong. I stayed the night and then took the train back into China, visited South China and boarded the train back to Hong Kong. I began to not feel well. Something was not right with me, but I knew I would be at the Hong Kong hotel soon.

I arrived at the hotel and tried to rest. It was not possible due to the pain, and I ended up at the front desk asking for a doctor. At that point, I knew I needed help. They arranged a taxi to take me to the hospital. I was in a lot of pain but doing my best to hold on. There was a lot of conversation with the Chinese folks that I could not understand. I tried to communicate with people that did not understand me. And then, a young person showed up and talked to me in English. I needed Hong Kong dollars for them to address my issues. I had some local dollars but they were way short of what was needed. Credit card was not accepted. The taxi driver remained there to take me back to the hotel, and he informed the hotel about my health situation. The Taxi driver then left and returned with enough money to get me seen by a doctor. *Wow, that was great as I needed help.* I was leaning against the wall waiting to be seen doing my best to fight off the pain and then, collapsed to my knees. I really thought I was done; I was exhausted and, in more pain, than I could handle, so if this was it, then fine. Then I passed out and fell to the floor.

The next thing I know I was in a hospital bed, tied down and unable to move. The doctor saw me struggling and ran over. He told me his name and could speak English well; he was a graduate from Stanford. He informed me that they tied me down because I had needles in my arm and they did not want me to wake up and hurt myself. He continued that one needle was to hydrate me, and the other was for pain. It was clear that I was exhausted, dehydrated, and I had a kidney stone. "I want you to take this little pill (it will help you sleep), and I will talk to you in the morning," he said. I was trying to get a grasp on where I was and how I got there, but took the pill and quickly fell asleep. The doctor was there when I woke up, and we agreed that I would have the kidney stone removed the next day via Lithotripsy. I would have to stay in the hospital another day or two and then could go on to Vietnam. Fortunately, a colleague that I was meeting with to visit Vietnam was able to get to the hospital and be with me. His efforts and care will always be remembered. It was a nice feeling to know that someone was there with me. He was able to rearrange our travel. All went well, and we were off to the production fields of Vietnam, just three days later than planned.

Moving Back to Idaho

Rebecca had already graduated high school and moved back to Idaho to attend Boise State, just like she promised she would. She was also working a job near Boise, and renting an apartment there. Our other three daughters remained in California; Terra was at the Heald Business School in Salinas; Carrie was at Fresno State, and Ashlie was attending Gavilan College in Gilroy. This year was a challenging year as all of our four daughters were attending college at the same time. We provided them with a vehicle and did not want them/us to be burdened with student loans so Lynette and I had to be resourceful. Lynette took a job with the Hollister School District, and I took on extra jobs whenever I could.

Now (Beginning of 2003), the company decided to move its main office to our location in Parma, Idaho. The thought of moving back to Idaho gave me the feeling like I was going home. This would uproot many families, but the company was thoughtful in its approach in moving those that were willing.

It wasn't exactly "home" just yet, though. As with any corporate move, many of us had to hit the ground running before re-planting our roots with our families. Some found homes right away, others took more time, and some of us decided to build our own houses. Our production manager, who was also moving to Idaho from California, was building a house and so was I. We had spent time working and staying together in Chile, so we already knew each other very well. We did what we needed to do because it made sense at the time. We lived in a house that the company had on one of their farms just across the border in Oregon. We were certainly no strangers to living in an old farm house. It's outdated carpet and pink curtains earned it our nickname "Shag Pad," but it nevertheless served our purpose.

Because she was already in Idaho, Rebecca was helping us look at houses and lots between Boise and Parma, where the company is located. If we were to consider buying property outside of a housing plan, we initially thought that an acre was all we wanted to build on because we didn't have time to take care of more land than that. We found a house we liked, but it was not in the location we preferred. The continued search brought us to a sloping thirteen acres north of Middleton that certainly caught my eye. It was located about forty minutes northwest of Boise. Rebecca and I went out to take a closer look at the property.

I could envision us building on one acre of that land and leaving the remaining twelve acres in alfalfa. I could see our home situated on the high end of the slope. The measurements of the home we found and liked fit the new location perfectly. The idea took hold of me, and I couldn't wait for Lynette to fly out to share my vision with her. Rebecca and I carefully marked off the house (and the shop I wanted to include) in a light snow with different colored flags so Lynette, who was flying out the next day, could get a clear understanding of what I wanted to do.

After the initial surprise of expecting to see a one-acre lot to now seeing thirteen acres laid out before her, it wasn't long before Lynette was on board with this new vision. I welcomed her solid suggestions about the placement of the shop in relation to the house, so I plotted out the shop north by twenty feet, and we flagged the yard and the fence area. Together, we made a few adjustments, but that plan remains the layout of our home today.

We bought the thirteen acres from a local family, and we found that we could build the house we wanted for less than the other places we were looking at. The builder we planned to hire was already building in the area and just happened to be the builder of the home we liked at the unacceptable location. *Wow, things were working out.*

Apparently, there was still one other order of business I had to tend to. My schedule was very tight as I was still immersed in international travel but the land owner approached me about needing to build a road on the north edge of the thirteen acres for access to the adjacent five acres.

The next order of business was a meeting with the local county road department as they wanted to know the name of the road. I respectfully told the owner that since this property had been in his family for years, I thought it should be named after his family. He appreciated my comment and said, "Okay, but they want an alternative as well. What if our name is not accepted?

We need a backup name just in case." I said, "Okay, if it's not going to be your name, it should be my name." "Is that Amarel Road? Or Amarel Lane?" he asked as he took notes. "Let's make it Amarel Way," I said with a grin, "since I like to think my way is the only way." He took the proposed names to the road department and reported back to me the next day that apparently there was a snag in using his name so "Amarel Way" it would be.

The sign had to be made and the pole installed. Since I was traveling and would be out of the country soon, I headed to the road department the next day. I had no idea what I got myself into but within a reasonable cost and time, our road sign was up. The whole process made me think back to Teele's Hardware when we first moved to Payette years earlier. That no-frills, honest, transparent way of dealing with others. It's things like this that make us want to be here.

In September of 2003, our house was completed. Over the years, we've expanded our property by purchasing the adjacent five acres, then adjacent twelve acres (now thirty acres in total) and adding a venue building "The Barn." The Barn has a certified kitchen used by Shurz Good (our Spices) and serves as a venue for Friends of Our Community (Our 501C3 that supports the Community). The thirty acres which remains mostly farmland includes our home, a shop, a storage shed, and The Barn – The place we call home.

GROWTH

"Watching something grow is good for
morale. It helps us believe in life."

— Myron S. Kaufmann

"If you are going to sell a product in the seed business you need
to know how to grow it . . . a company could sell a lot more if they
could educate the buyer and provide growing instructions."

— Rebecca Amarel, English Period 2, Travel Journal

Daughters' International Trips

Extensive international travel was my reality. Our daughters were growing up, soon to graduate high school and then be on their own. Starting with our oldest daughter Rebecca, it became a tradition to take each one of our daughters on an international trip with me when they graduated from high school; a trip of their choosing anywhere that was already on my business travel itinerary. Each daughter had their own separate trip. It was the perfect chance to show them the world, introduce them to other cultures, meet the people I work with, and create special memories of their own. I will forever treasure each and every one of those trips.

Unlike trips on my own, we took a little time for sightseeing. But they spent a lot of time in the fields. In fact, I'm sure they have a lot of stories to share about their trips and their father. Unless you have a lot of time, do not ask when they are all together as one topic will lead to another and the timeframe and topics may get out of hand.

Rebecca chose to go to Thailand with me. And while she was able to enjoy some of the sights of this amazing country, Rebecca was also out in the fields with me, meeting the locals and the company reps, and tasting the local foods. Mid-way through our trip, Rebecca wrote in her journal: "I'm learning a lot about the business life which is really great for me. I am looking forward now to going to college to study business or personnel." At the time, I had no idea what a powerful impression our trip left on her. Her English teacher's prerequisite for her excused absence was that she documents her daily impressions and experiences of Thailand. While her journal entries were credit-worthy for her teacher, Rebecca's impressions of our trip together were even more meaningful to me when she shared them with me at the end of our trip.

Terra traveled with me on one of my trips to France. The logistics of our trip couldn't have worked out better. When Terra was twelve years old, she used to babysit for the children of a local family we knew well. The family ended up moving to the French countryside and we reached out to them when I knew Terra would be traveling with me to France. They were excited to host her for a few days while I took care of company business in the area and then, went on to Israel. According to plan, Terra and I flew into Paris then on to Toulouse, rented a car, drove out of town, and headed for the countryside. We found their house and enjoyed a short visit as I dropped Terra off with them. I took care of business in the area and then drove back to the airport and flew to Israel. Surprisingly, I finished my work in Israel sooner than I had expected, so I told Terra that I'd be arriving to pick her up early. With the extra day we had, Terra and I toured the sights of Paris including the Louvre, Notre Dame, and the Eiffel Tower.

Carrie accompanied me on a trip to Holland and Italy. We left The Netherlands for Italy with a Dutch colleague, to visit the crops and deal with a personnel issue. We arrived in Bologna, and I took care of business in the area. We enjoyed some delicious meals, then headed south to Foggia to check the production there. We spent a day there with the local fieldman when they informed me that the personnel issue in the north was resurfacing again and needed my attention. Carrie and I took one of the most beautiful train rides along the Adriatic Sea, which took about five hours, back to northern Italy. When my business was completed, we returned to the company's main office in The Netherlands, and before returning to the US, we had a great time in Amsterdam that included a tour of the Anne Frank House.

Ashlie came with me to South Africa. After many hours of flying and waiting, we arrived in Oudtshoorn where we were finally able to get some good rest. The next day, we drove for six hours out to a remote location where the production was located. When we finally arrived at the farmer's house with the local representative, Ashlie was not feeling well. The farmer's wife graciously invited Ashlie into their home and took care of her while the farmer and I visited the fields. Some water, a little rest, and Ashlie was feeling alright. This kind of travel is rough if you are not used to it, but it is normal for seed production people. When Ashlie found out about the Cango Wildlife Ranch just north of Oudtshoorn, she wanted to visit there. She wanted to "pet the cheetahs." I was nervous, but if she wanted to go, I wasn't about to let her go in there alone. She absolutely loved it (and I was happy to have this as part of our trip behind us). Taking my daughters on their trips at the end of high school was perfect timing; they were old enough to appreciate the experiences, the people, and the culture. Plus, they were moving on to college and creating lives of their own. I realized that their schedules would soon be filled with other activities, places, and people in their lives. Even though respected, Mom and Dad would become a lesser part of their lives. Lynette initially expressed to me how sad she was that the girls were each leaving for college. Yes, I was sad as well. But we agreed, while we wanted our daughters to be close to us always, it would be unfair to think how their absence would affect us. We would rather consider the opportunity and support them in every way we can.

Instead of being sad that our daughters were leaving home, we decided to celebrate this day for them. This is a time in their lives when they must go out on their own; it's a growth point they must experience, and an opportunity they can't pass up. They should go discover their lives, go out on their own, and meet people. If we handled it any other way, then we wouldn't be helping them to grow or serving them the best that we could.

Flight to Amsterdam

I'd flown to Amsterdam so many times, I lost count. I always stayed at a hotel near Roermond, Netherlands (right on the border of Germany). In fact, one of the waiters at the hotel restaurant asked me one night, how many days I had stayed at that hotel because, according to his count, I was always there. He was a nice and pleasant person that would take some time for me when not busy. I normally do not keep track of how long I have been traveling but I then started to figure it out and was a little surprised. For five months straight, I stayed more nights in this hotel than my own home. Even though it was against my rule of counting my travel days, this was reality. In fact, when employees would complain about their travel—I have missed this many weekends, worked these many holidays and this many extra hours—I would tell them, "I understand that we have to manage our travel and our personal time, but I think the best thing you can do to help yourself is enjoy where you are, enjoy the people you are with, and stop counting the days your away from home." I was recently amazed and honored when a good friend in the seed business mentioned that he remembers and uses this advice even today.

However, one particular flight to Amsterdam turned out to be the eventful. I happened to be seated next to a gentleman whose advice expanded the boundaries of my management philosophy, and whose perspectives caused me to unlock truths about my own personality that I needed to change, in order to pave the way to further success. In short, the person I sat next to on that particular flight not only translated a management style into a lifestyle, he became a friend and an influential person in my life.

I boarded the plane for Amsterdam, settling into my seat with all intentions of working on my strategic plan for operations in anticipation of my trip. I greeted the gentleman who was seated next to me. We seemed to hit it off and began talking about our jobs, our families, where we were heading, and why.

I'm always inclined to talk to people I sit next to. My daughters have told me that I don't know any strangers. But this conversation was easy and relaxed. I felt like I had known him forever despite the fact that we had never met before. We were both interested in what the other had to say, and there was something about him that really resonated with me.

I learned that he was the founder and CEO of a proven leadership training method called Pathways to Leadership. And here I was, coincidentally, working on my strategic business plan. We had a long conversation about management style and the type of training his company provided. His philosophy echoed my code of honesty, transparency, communication, and relationship-building. We shared the belief in honoring others' concerns and points of view. He explained his beliefs and included his approach and tools to support them. His company has provided training that was very valuable and meaningful, but somehow, this seemed different.

As our plane was landing, he wrote his contact information on a card, together with some notes we discussed, titles of the books he had written, and gave it to me so we could stay in touch. I provided him with my business card.

When I got back home, I told Lynette and Rebecca (who was living with us at that time) about the fascinating guy I met on the plane. When I mentioned his name, Rebecca immediately made the connection, disappeared into her room and returned with one of his books she had to read for one of her college assignments at Boise State. When she presented me with his book, it was clear to me, "Yes! That's him!"

He reached out to me some time after our flight and invited me to his upcoming wedding in Denver. I remember telling Lynette, "Let's accept the invitation. Although I don't know him very well, he sure is an interesting guy, and I can't deny that I have a connection with him." At the time, I was in California, and Lynette was at home in Idaho. I arranged flights so that Lynette and I would meet in Denver for the wedding. It was an amazing evening, and we were welcomed there like we were family. During this visit we had a conversation that became reality when my son-in-law, Richard and I joined him on a hiking excursion to the top of Longs Peak. A challenging hike that was full of conversation, lessons, and experiences.

As Director of Global Operations and US Country Head, I worked closely with our HR department. I enthusiastically told the HR manager about the Pathways training which I wanted to incorporate into the company. I could tell from that conversation; I was more enthusiastic about the topic than her.

I did not want to give up the opportunity and reached out for ideas. The proposal: He would find a way for us to sit in on a current training, just to experience it for ourselves. We agreed, and we both attended a trial training at different locations.

What I witnessed at the training was surprising. People were opening up, showing their passion, and the emotion that was triggered by the manner and questions that were asked. They paid attention to their feelings and those of their coworkers. Expressing your true feelings lowers your guard. When that happens, you're more willing to listen and cooperation comes more easily. When everyone feels like they're heard and considered in the process, they are more willing. Personal and professional lives merge, uplifting everyone to become not only more productive, but to become better people with an elevated quality of life.

After these trial training sessions, we agreed there was something unique in these trainings. We received training for talent, knowledge, and behavior which was great, needed, and very beneficial, but this was different.

I moved on to get my global team scheduled for the new training. Coming from different places in the world, we all gathered for our session. We began by building on our company goals, operational objectives, and personal targets. Our style, feelings, and passion were taken into consideration, in a way that was never emphasized before.

At the last session, one of the guys on our global team made it a point to walk over afterward to thank me. Helping the company, he said, was one thing. But taking these tools of openness, honesty, and respecting the feelings of others home to my family helped him personally as well. He continued while I stood there, emotionally moved to hear what he had to say.

Our training undoubtedly brought us closer together, and we left feeling like a team really; our opinions and feelings counted, and so did each of our colleagues'. I knew my team members now much better than I did before our training session.

This helped me to hone my management skills by understanding that when we're faced with an issue, we have a tool box that contains the tools needed. We have to assess the situation, realize what we want to accomplish, understand the tools we need to accomplish it, reach in and grab them, then start applying them.

It all boils down to caring and awareness—awareness of ourselves and of others. Being aware of personality traits, knowing what you want to accomplish, and asking the right questions to involve others in the plan and find the appropriate solution. This will take some thought, but it's worth the time.

Being able to combine the training from Advance Business Consulting and Pathways, I was able to build my own style and management tools. I have a lot of respect for these trainings and the value they provide. I have learned that taking the personal styles in mind and posing a few insightful questions yield a wealth of information that's useful at many levels.

Discovery

The company was expanding and needed to update its operating system. A team was put together. Needs, requirements, and a manager of the project was identified. Because operations were a big part of the project, I and members of the operations team were included. This was a huge global change of the software system. A couple attempts were made but fell short of being successful. The project manager decided to leave the company, and the CEO wanted to elevate the manager to a board position. I was asked to take on the project, but I knew this was a big stretch for me. With the CEO's backing and support of the current system manager, I took on the task. A lot of meetings and details, and even an external project manager was hired to assist the project. We had a lot of success, but some challenges remained. I wanted to bring everyone together to work out the details and solve these problems. This would be a meeting where all involved would be in attendance and solutions would be found for the remaining unsolved issues. The meeting became a political one; some thought we were not ready for the meeting, and some thought it was not needed at all. I was committed to getting everyone in one place and not leave until the problems were solved. This meeting was held in June and came to be known as the "The June Meeting." Held in The Netherlands with all pertinent people from multiple countries in attendance. The meeting was challenged as some tried to stop it from happening. I will always be grateful for the continued support of the CEO and his belief in me. I remember, I had a meeting with him as he coached me to not let the emotions overrule the facts and results. We agreed to put everything on the table, sweep off the emotions and work with the facts.

The meeting participates split up to discuss the challenges within each group and then came together to see how their solutions fit into the overall project. There came a point when the challenges were challenged. The few that thought the meeting was not needed and not providing solutions, raised to a point of rejection.

The external project manager was assisting me. He had just attended a meeting with one of the managers in rejection and wanted to end the meeting. He provided his reasons and I strongly disagreed. I did not want to hear why we had to stop, but wanted to hear solutions and ways to continue. He then told me that he could not support continuing the meeting. *Are we done? Another failure? I was now bewildered and at my wits end.* At this point in the game, I knew who to ask for support. I met with a few of the managers and the CEO Then, I informed the project manager that I respected his opinion and decision to not continue. Therefore, the meeting would continue without him. I then attended the meeting of the manger in rejection and found that his team was willing and with an open approach that included their ideas, solutions were possible. I then continued to meet with other groups. A couple had their issues resolved, and the others were making progress.

In the end, the June Meeting was the turning point of the project that was implemented successfully in five countries and then came to become the global system of the company. To me, this was a great example of success that was made possible by dedicated people gathering for a common goal.

School in India

Out of all my travels, a few places immediately stand out and for me; India is one of them. The people are welcoming, the culture is rich, and my experiences there are well beyond what I could ever imagine. It all prompted me to carry on my love for the people, and my desire to help others to do better in their lives.

When I was in India, we spent our time in the countryside where the fields were located—together with the local representatives, observing and interacting with the farmers and their workers. When possible, I would visit the local village where the people lived. I saw that they had virtually no possessions to speak of, yet they were happy with what they had. They were always so gracious to welcome me with a smiling face and an eager desire to communicate and relate. Those experiences humbled me. It is clear that the people in the villages don't have much, but they are happy with the few things they have.

The company established a bridge school near one of our main production areas. That school was the company's valiant effort to support the children in the area with a structured system that would provide them with education and, more importantly, training for opportunities they may otherwise not have.

I was greatly impressed with the company for making this happen and inspired by the mission. With this in mind, I questioned myself, "How can I personally support this effort?

To this day, together with the generous and the mindful assistance of the local people, we do our best to support the students. I appreciate all those that make this happen. I realize, I am only a small part of the process. Together, we make a good team, committed to the same cause. When I expressed my desire to support the mission, I was welcomed by those involved and wanting to be involved. Their support meant a lot to me.

One of the best gifts for these students is to teach them to be self-sufficient and financially independent. Providing them with the means to hone a skill or develop a trade to enhance their opportunities for earning a living is a blessing to them. The local team is always looking for ways to improve and provide for the children. Lynette and I were asked to support the purchase of sewing machines for the students at school. The students are trained in how to use the machines and, more importantly, how to use their skills into creating a business of their own.

Lynette and I were overwhelmed when we read the testimonials from the young girls at the school:

"My parents are happy for me, and I feel very confident that I can lead the family and support it in all possible means."

"I am very much thankful to Ron and his family for helping me stand on my own two feet, and I wish to continue the tailoring even after my marriage."

The whole idea behind what we do is to enable others to do better in their lives.

Not often, but sometimes, we're fortunate enough to get a glimpse of the significance of our help. On my trip to India, we arrived and they took us to the school. A reception line as formed. We were able to meet and talk to each student individually. I was glad that Rebecca's husband, Richard, was able to join me on this trip.

I was informed that one student wanted to meet me when we arrived. They told me she wasn't feeling well, but she specifically wanted to meet me and then, had to return home. I remember she greeted us in a weakened condition but with a big smile. We shared a few words, and she went on her way. I did not know why she was ill, but it was so nice of her to make the special effort to meet us.

During a meeting at the end of my visit, they provided me a status report and informed me how the donations were being spent. After the normal expenses of books and other essential needs, there was money left for other expenses. That money was diverted to another cause, they told me. When I asked why, they informed me that the young lady who wanted to meet me when I arrived was recuperating from stomach surgery to remove a tumor. The money for the other expenses was used for her operation.

Wow. I quietly and humbly responded, "What a great decision."

Friends of Our Community

There are two sayings that our family lives by: "Earn your keep," and "Help those who help others." With the love and support of my family and friends, we've integrated both principles into the development and initiation of Friends of Our Community. Friends of Our Community was founded to support the community in which we live and pay back in a way to help others.

Just like its name sounds, Friends of Our Community is designed to help people who help others and, in the process, to strengthen our community bonds. It's our way of contributing to our community and strengthening the chain of life.

Friends of Our Community lives, breathes, and grows through the love and support of like-minded people who share our vision and our mission. Greatly appreciated are our friends and family that help us make all of this happen.

Through Friends of Our Community, we provide food, cooking and catering services. We griddle pancakes and sausages for breakfasts and grill on a wood fired barbecue, hamburgers, hot dogs, tri-tip and/or chicken for a variety of events that support the health of our community. In the spring and fall we host, at "The Barn", a gathering of friends and neighbors we call a "Date Night." Date Night brings everyone together for great food and entertainment. You never know what is going to happen that night as the plan can change as we go, depending on the crowd. A movie, a football game, and /or other off the wall games and interaction.

To me, rodeo represents the American West and is "The All-American Sport." Therefore, we support rodeos when we can. With that in mind, I've developed what we call "The Rope of Hope." The Rope of Hope is a small red, white and blue colored lasso, and with some instruction and practice, anyone can learn to spin it.

We also introduced The Rope of Hope for an event we hosted for the Leukemia/Lymphoma Society with the slogan: "Every turn of the rope secures a cure for cancer." All the proceeds from the sales of The Rope of Hope went to support cancer research.

The Rope of Hope was taken with us to the Jordan Valley Rodeo BBQ. We needed help getting our message out to the crowd. We elicited the help of a couple of young gentlemen (ten to twelve years of age) to get the word out about our ropes and their significance. What happened next, I will never forget.

One of the kids asked a friend to help him sell these ropes; his friend asked, "What is in it for me?" His question was answered in a heartbeat, "What you get out from this, is the good feeling you get in your heart knowing that you helped someone." The words of a twelve-year-old boy that could not have been expressed better. Those kids were dedicated and enthusiastic as, in only minutes later, I heard the rodeo emcee announce, The Rope of Hope was available for sale, as he proudly explained the meaning and significance of The Rope of Hope. They sold all we had.

The Rope of Hope at the "Light the Night" event for the Leukemia/ Lymphoma Society. It was a large event with the Boise State Cheerleaders making an appearance. I was helping coach a young man spin The Rope of Hope. I could tell he was challenged, but I patiently kept working with him and after some attempts, he got it! He could spin The Rope of Hope all by himself. When his mother witnessed what was happening, she patiently observed and then, approached us literally with tears in her eyes exclaiming, "Do you know what you've just done?" She went on to explain that her son was not capable of doing such a feat, but, "After just a few tries, you got him to spin that rope on his own!" Wow, I had no idea, but I told her it was all him; I was just supporting his effort. His mother complimented him for his success, and he was awarded a Rope of Hope.

Needless to say, I like to stay busy. I've developed an allergic reaction to laziness, dishonesty, and selfishness, so I surround myself with people who don't make me sick. Also, I have learned that standing up for what you believe in can create challenges and some sleepless nights.

I fully believe we were blessed with:

Eyes for seeing,

Ears for listening,

Mouth for communicating,

Hands for doing,

Legs for moving,

Brain for creating,

Heart for caring,

Gut for feeling,

Soul for believing.

I hope that I can effectively utilize these blessings to support others. For me, making this happen supports "Earning your Keep." Also, spending six years on the Idaho Commerce Advisory Council and other Local Services brought some great insight regarding the need for Friends of our Community in our state and communities.

Future

I am not sure what retiring would really look like for me, but since getting out of the corporate world in 2019, I've had more time to devote to growing my own ideas and endeavors. I'm putting my imagination, creativity, and experience to good use by expanding on my ideas.

To make this happen I launched R & L Consulting, I intended it to be an agricultural consulting business. Interestingly enough, my first clients were not in agriculture at all. Since management skills can easily transfer across different fields, I was more than happy to assist a couple companies outside of my intended scope.

Now, I'm working with agricultural clients in the US and internationally as well—seed business consulting, organic seed treatments, and soil additives that I've trialed and experimented with, in the fields and in my own rudimentary lab.

For a time, I worked with my uncle in the soil amendment business. I really enjoyed the time that him and I spent together learning and reacquainting myself with him, my aunt and getting to know their family even more.

Seed MC is another project I'm currently working on. The concept is a cloud-based seed production management software that can be accessed from any device. The project is currently expanding and has caught the attention of some major players in the seed business.

Another project on the horizon is SEE Scope. SEE stands for Seed Examination Equipment and Scope refers to a microscope. Essentially, the idea is to pay more attention to the seed. This allows seed conditioning, seed treatment, or whoever it may be to actually see the intricacies of the seed on a microscopic level, easily on a screen.

And then there is Shurz Good Spices. A family blend of spices we have used for many years when we BBQ. This is Friends of Our Community's spices of choice that are now bottled under the brand of Shurz Good Spices.

Right now, I'm as busy as I want to be.

I keep thinking about my first lesson in the seed business. "Pay attention to the seed." With today's technology, we can make this happen in ways not imagined previously with more advanced technology on the way.

I know, at times, it is best to leave things to others and not get involved. However, if I see a need, not getting involved is a difficult task for me. If asked, "What do I need help with?" I am sure Lynette would say, "What about patience? I think help is needed there." Now that is the kind of openness and honesty I like. (Loving input)

At one point in my career, I remember telling my coworkers that our boss was like a rocket with a tremendous amount of fuel. His ideas were going to take off no matter what. It was up to us to steer that rocket in the right direction so it doesn't crash and burn.

I hope I have the right amount of fuel and guidance to make my ideas a success.

Mokie Bear

When my girls were young (aged eight, six, four, and four), Lynette and I took them to Disneyland for Easter. While driving, in the spirit of Easter, I made up a story that they all remember and refer to even today. I wanted this story to live in our family, so, Mokie the Bear was created.

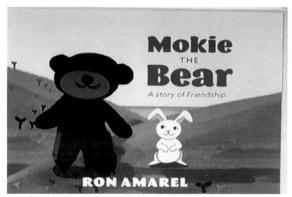

Mokie the Bear
A Story of Friendship

Mokie the Bear by Ron Amarel
BookShop (bookbaby.com)

HARVEST

"Talk unbelief, and you will have unbelief; but talk faith, and you will have faith. According to the seed sown will be the harvest."

— ELLEN G. WHITE

"Your character is the harvest of your habits."

— ADRIAN ROGERS

Boating

I agree with the belief: work hard, play hard. To me, the harvest in your life are the successes you make in work and with your family. It's a time to be thankful and to count your blessings. I am sure there were times when my body asked my mind, *what were you thinking?* In return, my mind would respond, *I thought you were better than that.* Riding bulls, buffalos, and water skiing in freezing temperatures is maybe not for everyone.

July 4, 1977 was the first "4th of July" holiday Lynette and I spent together as a married couple. "Okay, it is the 4th of July," she says, "we always spend that at the lake; so, let's go." Well, I was approaching the peak of hay season, but expected to be at the lake. Like normal, when you are married, things have to be worked out. Lynette left with her family for a two-week vacation at the lake, and I stayed back baling hay. In an effort to express my flexibility and understanding, I worked extra hours so I could join them at the weekend, before their vacation ended. I realized first-hand how much fun having a boat could be.

As time went on, I was able to save enough to purchase a boat and keep up the tradition. When I bought our first boat, I wanted it to be large enough for the six of us, so the girls could learn how to waterski. After owning a couple of boats, I decided to expand our capabilities to wake boarding and wake surfing. I then decided on a Malibu Wake Setter which we named "Ooga Mooska" after Hank Thompson's song, *"Squaws Along the Yukon"* (Ooga, Ooga Mooska—which means I love you).

Since our daughters were in grade school, I would turn on the stereo every morning and play music to wake them up. They grew up with a mix of music that included Rock, Soul and Country Western, so they didn't blink an eye when we played *"Squaws Along the Yukon"* from the boat's loud speakers every time Ooga Mooska left the dock. It became our boat's theme song.

As the years have gone by, we've enjoyed wake surfing, wake boarding, swimming, and waterskiing. We're carrying on the tradition of boating with our grandchildren as well –teaching them how to fish, swim, and enjoy water sports. I am now giving hydrofoils a try.

Harley - Rendezvous in Winnemucca

When we first moved to Hollister, it was actually Lynette who encouraged me to buy a Harley- Davidson bike. Hollister, California is well known for its annual July 4th bike rallies. I've always enjoyed riding a motorcycle. Last year, I changed my tune a bit when I started out for a three-day ride to Wisconsin, despite a storm rolling in. After riding for two hours, the storm was getting worse, so I rode back home and cancelled my trip. Disappointed, but it made sense to cancel. Getting older, getting wiser, maybe? I now curtail my riding a bit, but that long haul on a good day is still in my sights.

In the summer of 2012, Tim, who worked with me when I first started my hay business, wanted to do the Iron Butt Challenge ride, i.e., ride your motorcycle one thousand miles in twenty-four hours. As he was trying to convince me to go with him, Tim told me that I was the only guy he knew who was crazy enough to say yes to the challenge. Yes, I was flattered, and I thanked him for his confidence in me? I did accept the challenge, and we had a great trip together. We also received our iron butt patch.

Rodeo

It was June in 2010 at the Nyssa Night Rodeo as Lynette, Rebecca, and I watched the rodeo. This is when I decided and made the decision that I would ride one more time before I turned sixty years old. I'm not sure why but the thought came to me so strong and clear that I knew I would make it true. As the year progressed, the desire became stronger and as the day got closer, I knew I would ride a buffalo. Lynette did not understand, "I have no idea why you think you have to do this, but I know if your mind is made up, you will do it, no matter what I say." I'm not sure why she took this attitude as I usually try to listen and be flexible. You can ask anyone of my daughters. When they were challenged with a project or wanting to get something done, I would tell them, "Do as you please as long as you do it the way I want you to." Now that is flexibility, right?

A member of the company's finance team (a brave and adventurous young man) was willing to ride as well. He had never ridden before and even though I wondered why he wanted to join me in the challenge, I should not ask and only support him anyway I could.

For those that have never rodeoed, it is more of a team sport than you would ever know. The riders supporting each other, sharing experiences, knowledge, and equipment, knowing that when the gate opens, it is between you and the animal.

The day of the rodeo, we were behind the chutes. The buffalos seemed bigger than those years before. We reminded ourself that we were doing this for a good cause as we promoted and took pledges to benefit breast cancer patients. Our goal was to make at least $6,000, and we came very close to meeting our goal.

I had a weak shoulder that bothered me from time to time, originally injured in a rodeo when I was in college; I am sure. Yes, I was one of the those crazy, adrenaline junkies, a bull rider. However, in those days, the party after made all the effort and soreness worth it.

Well, the buffalo ride was shorter than I wanted as I came off on my shoulder. Yes, I handled it like a cowboy, *"Deal with it and move on as there is no time for sympathy, and I'd never ask for any, anyway."*

During my hay hauling days, I injured my knee, and it was something I dealt with until now. However, something caused it to shoot a pain in the joint that was unbearable. At this point, I decided to have it fixed and made an appointment to see a doctor. I told the doctor that my knee was an issue, but while I was there, my shoulder too could be looked at. X-rays were completed on both. The doctor's comment was, "I'm not sure what the knee problem is, but that shoulder needs to be fixed." His advice was taken seriously, and I asked if I could have them both fixed at the same time. The discussion began upon his disagreement. I was busy, and I did not want to go to the hospital twice. In the end, we did them both at the same time. This was in December, so I had the winter break to heal. My knee was not too bad, and I was able to walk on it, but my shoulder was a little painful. My shoulder was a rotator cuff, but they also had to fix the connection of the clavicle to the shoulder blade. The doctor said it was broken before and attached itself via cartilage. Yes, they broke it off, cleaned the cartilage, and then, pinned it back correctly. So, my shoulder is fixed, and I can walk. Prayers were answered, but I had no idea of the unanswered prays until future X-rays of my shoulder to evaluate its healing. The X-ray technician, what a great person he was, noticed a shadow in the X-ray. He brought it to the attention of the doctor on call.

I was changing into my clothes, ready to go home after the X-rays, when I was informed to, stay in the gown. There seemed to be some confusion, so I needed to hang out. I was not sure what was happening, but they were holding me here at the hospital. As mentioned earlier, patience is not one of my virtues, but I remember thinking that you have to trust and believe in others as they may know better than you. This was for sure the case, at this time. The doctor came in and informed me that they wanted to admit me overnight for observation. I called Lynette and she headed my way. They set me up in a room and when she arrived, the doctor was there. He apologized for the wait and unclarity, but they needed to discuss the issue with a specialist in Boise. "The fact is, we have found an aneurism in your chest that is serious. An Aorta Aneurism that has dilated to 4.8, so we can discuss it with you," the doctor told my wife. *Wow*, I felt fine and they say I am in critical condition. *What?* I was handed a cell phone to talk to the specialist myself. I informed him that I had plans to fly to Chile the next day and asked him what we could do about that. He informed me that I was not traveling to Chile as I was going to spend a couple days in the hospital. He explained that if I was dilated to 5.0, we would not be talking and as he would be preparing for an emergency surgery, but I was at 4.8, so we could hold off and run some tests. I had to agree to stay in the hospital and relax. And then, he told me, "Here is my prognosis: go on and live your life as is and I give you, at the most six months to live. Become a couch potato and I give you two years. Fix this thing and go on about your life. And, by the way, I could be wrong about the six months; it could be tomorrow."

I spent that night in the hospital, and the next day, they wanted me to see for myself the X-rays of what they found. They asked if some medical students could join us to review the X-rays? I said, "Why not, I have nothing to hide." We went into the examination room, and they joined us. It was then that I understood the urgency of this as the doctor explained how this was a very rare moment when the X-rays can be viewed with the students and the patient in the same room. In times before, the patient had passed on and therefore, was not present in the room. After this meeting, it was time to talk to the specialist again for an update on his opinion. He informed me that after more review, while I was at 4.8, he was going to allow me to go home as long as I agreed to rest and come back the next day for some more tests. He wanted to do some tests of my arteries along with a scope of the heart.

Wow, I have to call someone from my management team as they are at the Boise Airport, probably wondering where I am. I was able to reach them and informed them of my situation.

Things seem to be moving fast. I am now in a Boise Hospital and the doctor brought me the news. I wanted to test your heart because if we have to fix the aneurism, we should also complete any by-passes if needed. The good news is that my heart and arteries are all in good shape and overall, I am in good shape, but I still have this aneurism. He explained my timeline once more and then made a pretty convincing comment. He said, "You understand the issues and that you need to get this fixed, but if you have not made up your mind yet, I just want to add that without a fix, sex is no longer allowed." With that comment, I told him that I had only one question, "When can we get this fixed?" I was there for tests. He said he would get back to me in an hour or so.

He came back and informed me that he had a cancelation and I should stay in the hospital to prepare for surgery "Day after tomorrow, let's do it," he said.

The day was here, they came to prepare me and gave me a sedative. At that point I thought, *Wow, I know that if I am allowed to wake up at the end of this I will hurt for a while, but the alternative did not seem acceptable, so please give me the strength to endure.* I remember being in deep thought at that time and thinking, *what if I did not ride the buffalo? Why was I so determined to do so?* Then, a nurse came to talk to me. It felt like I knew her because she looked and even talked like a lady I previously worked with. This lady was a strong believer in angels and that was a satisfying thought as I dosed off. Work has been my life; now, work has found a way to reach out to me when I needed it. Could that be true? I do not think that everyone should ride a buffalo, but you should not be afraid of taking a chance in life or afraid of following your intuition. Know your limits, stretch them, if possible, and go for it. Nothing happens without a jolly good positive effort.

After the surgery, the same nurse was there, and I asked Lynette if I was going crazy? Please tell me who this nurse reminds you of. Comfort was provided with her agreement. So here I was. I came in feeling well, but they said I was broken. Now, I feel broken, and they say I am doing well. Hard to understand life sometimes.

All went pretty well, and I was home in three days. The doctor told me that this surgery would take away my stamina and that I would have to build it back up. *Okay, I was in pretty good shape before the surgery, so I could bounce back pretty fast*, I thought, *in fact, it was not long ago that I hiked to the top of Longs Peak.* That was a great experience that was riskier than I ever knew. Well, the day finally came when they allowed me to ride a stationary bike or the elliptical. Before, I was doing both for thirty minutes each. I could not do more than two minutes on the elliptical. *So, if that is the way it's going to be, I will deal with that*, I thought, and I set a goal: 1.5 minutes tomorrow and increase it 15 seconds every day. In a few weeks, I was good to go and felt much better. Like many things in my life, it challenged my commitment and determination. Without self-discipline, a reasonable target, and the help from others (mostly the loving care provided by Lynette), the goal would not have been achieved.

Heart of Idaho Award

Our daughter, Rebecca, earned the title of Mrs. Star (referring to the town she lived in about twenty miles northwest of Boise) and in 2015, she had participated in the Mrs. Idaho pageant.

Each year, the Mrs. Idaho pageant presents The Heart of Idaho Award to a member of the community who "inspires others by demonstrating extraordinary courage, faith, and love." Nominations are accepted by submitting a letter describing how the nominee has inspired others. The recipient of the award is named at the Mrs. Idaho pageant ceremony.

Without telling me beforehand, Rebecca nominated us for the 2015 Heart of Idaho Award. She drafted the requisite letter and submitted it, putting her emphasis on the work we were doing in the community and the school in India.

Rebecca wanted to make sure I was going to be at the pageant because she knew I was going to get the award. I had no idea until my name was called, but being nominated by our daughter and winning that award was one of the best surprises of my life. I was honored to have won, but even more honored to know that our daughters respect our vision and the work we accomplished on behalf of others.

2015 Heart of Idaho Recipient

Ron Amarel

Nominated by Rebecca Stonhill, Mrs Star 2015

Founder of Friends of Our Community. A non–profit organization developed to fulfill a promise. God help me be successful and provide for our family. If I can just be successful, I PROMISE to give back.☐ www.friendsofourcommunity.com

Something that started out as personal challenge of remote cooking for the company, field days have created the know-how and ability for us to serve many. Twenty-seven hundred people were the most we ever served in one night. Friends of Our Community was privileged to participate at an annual Boise event - Light the Night.

We've participated in local events like St. Luke's MSTI (Mountain States Tumor Institute) event. We've also supported schools. We have also supported the Make a Wish foundation by taking pledges for water skiing on January 1st. Our New Year's celebration was on the water for many years. Some years were more challenging than the others. The last time we participated, I took a picture of my vehicle thermometer, grabbed my ski, and jumped into the water. Now, this may be that adrenaline junky thing, as the air temperature was negative 6 degrees Fahrenheit. The ski went well as I skied right up to the shore, stepped out of the water and tried to remove my ski to join back with the others. With some help, I was able to break the ice away from the ski boot and remove my ski.

We have also supported local schools and fire departments with their needs for equipment like, Jaws of Life, Sim Man, and even a fire truck.

We also enjoy cooking breakfasts. The largest breakfast we ever served was for the Future Farmers of America (FFA) where about 1,100 people were fed that morning. We typically made pancakes and sausages. For those who asked for eggs, I assured them that they were in the pancakes! People are still surprised by how quickly, thoroughly, and efficiently we can set up to accommodate a crowd, and when done, be loaded up and on the way home.

We have the most dedicated team anyone could ask for. Friends and family are the backbone of Friends of Our Community, and it couldn't happen without their continued dedication, love and support. Rebecca's husband, Richard, together with some friends, Jeff, Shane and his father, Fred, and I do most of the cooking. Lynette, Rebecca, her son Reid and Denise, help with the preparation and serving. Lynette, Rebecca, Reid, Richard, Shane,

Fred, Jeff, and Denise have always played an integral part in Friends of Our Community. Just ask any of them for help and they're right there. I happily and proudly surround myself with people who love to be involved and commit themselves to the task. I could not ask for better than this.

Depending on time and resources, we offer our services and The Barn, in support of local fire departments, schools, organizations, and causes.

I guess you could say, the events my family and I host are our own version of the "Festas" I remember. Good food and drink provide the perfect setting, while family and community are at the heart of what we celebrate. People together, enjoying each other.

CONCLUSION

As I think back to my start in the seed business, I realize the influence and support I was provided by my loving wife and family. How they influenced my life before my career even began, and how they enabled me to be the best person I could be. (I realize improvement is still needed) On one of those training sessions, in the beginning of my career with my Southern Gentleman friend, I was presented with this poem that made an impression on me.

A Package of Seeds

I paid a dime for a package of seeds
And the clerk tossed them out with a flip.
"We've got 'em assorted for every man's needs,"
He said with a smile on his lip,
"Pansies and poppies and asters and peas!
Ten cents a package! And pick as you please!"
Now seeds are just dimes to the man in the store,
And the dimes are the things that he needs;
And I've been to buy them in seasons before,
But have thought of them merely as seeds.
But it flashed through my mind as I took them this time,
"You have purchased a miracle here for a dime!"
"You've a dime's worth of power which no man can create,
You've a dime's worth of life in your hand!
You've a dime's worth of mystery, destiny, fate,
Which the wisest cannot understand.
In this bright little package, now isn't it odd!
You've a dime's worth of something known only to God."

— EDGAR A. GUEST

I greatly appreciate the people I have worked with. They provided me with openness, understanding, diligence, training, and most of all, friendship and companionship.

I want to thank Pathways to Leadership and Advance Business Consulting for their training and patience with me. I was fortunate and appreciate the time they took to help me build, understand, and execute, what I think, was a successful management style and approach.

As I contemplate my life, beyond my professional career, I see the importance of the chain of life and greatly appreciate people that believed in me.

The best way I can describe it is this:

"**God put us here to be someone.**
To be someone you have to do something.
To do something you have to help someone.
And pray that the chain never breaks."

Ron Amarel